# Uncovering the Unconscious: A Course in Self Transformation

Mardi Horowitz, M.D.

Publication Design by Sherri Ortegren
Cover art by Mardi Horowitz

While the author has made every effort to provide accurate telephone numbers and Internet addresses at the time of publication, neither the publisher nor the author assumes any responsibility for errors, or for changes that occur after publication. Further, the publisher does not have any control over and does not assume any responsibility for author or third-party websites or their content.

ISBN: 1470013428
ISBN-13: 978-1470013424

# DEDICATION

*For Renée Binder, with love*

# Contents

# *Preface*

Just as playwrights use scripts to share stories with their audience, I have written this book to share what I have learned about the coherence and continuity of a person's sense of identity. And just as a theatrical script offers detailed directions on staging a play properly, this book offers guidance on solidifying your sense of who you really are. Consider it a valuable guide as you seek to reduce feelings of confusion, shame, guilt, envy, greed, and self-disgust while increasing your self-esteem and ability to care for others.

*Identity* means continuity in selfhood. We are the same in our present moments as we were before. Yet we know we can change in body, mind, and circumstances. Consciously, we want to prepare for future stresses, integrate past traumas into our realistic expectations for the present, and make good changes in our personal narrative about who we are and who we may yet become. In short, our conscious desire is to plan how best to meet our responsibilities, pursue our goals, avoid threats, and increase our satisfaction.

What we want consciously is not always the same as what we intend, expect, or desire unconsciously. And we have only partial conscious control over our unconscious attitudes. Using that partial control, we can reframe and augment our most reasonable plans for the future. We can confront and revise our distorting fears and become more optimistic. This usually means taking a middle path between our irrational aversions and our ideal expectations.

In my more than 40 years as a private-practice psychiatrist and a professor of psychiatry at the University of California, San Francisco, I've worked with thousands of individuals as they've searched for greater meaning and harmony in their lives. Through the years, I've observed again and again that there's no shortcut to happiness; there's only the voyage itself — the hard and fascinating work of finding a harmonious balance in our ideas about who we are and reaching an inner peace and satisfaction that underlies it. Putting our own sense of self in order can be hard work, but it is the most important work of all.

In this book, concepts related to a coherent sense of positive identity make up the core. The three chapters of Part I deal with just that: how self-attributions lead to a better sense of identity as we mature. The theater of the mind contains characters that represent, at different times, multiple possible selves — several personas, if you will. Increased self-understanding can affect how well these selves are brought together, perhaps by activating an inner chairperson. By better developing a conscious "self as decision maker" within, we can change our goals, attitudes, personal values, and plans for how to enhance our capacities.

Most of us can augment self-esteem by modifying unrealistic expectations and can gain respect — even love — by improving our relationships. People reflect back to us who we are, and our attachments to some of them stabilize our essential identity. To clarify ourselves, we can look into our minds for models of our relationships. That is the focus of the three chapters of Part II.

Changing our ideas about who we are means transforming the beliefs in which selfhood is embedded. We can process, reappraise, and modify our attitudes about ourselves and social relationships. Part III centers on that. The four chapters there show you how to amplify and use self-observations, and even how to access the sometimes nonconscious potential for emotional experiences that you both fear and desire — and, thus, avoid.

This book is written for the general reader, so I avoid cumbersome references and proofs of my assertions. Relevant resources are listed at the end. If you want more science, see my books *Person Schemas and Maladaptive Interpersonal Patterns; States of Mind: Personality Styles and Brief Psychotherapy; Introduction to Psychodynamics: A New Synthesis; Cognitive Psychodynamics: From Conflict to Character, Stress Response Syndromes, 5th edition*; and *Understanding Psychotherapy Change: A Practical Guide to Configurational Analysis*. On the other hand, if you want a short, practical book also for the general reader, look to my book *A Course in Happiness*.

As the curtain rises on your quest for self transformation, you will undoubtedly encounter both challenges and joys. You will perhaps struggle to find your place among the cast of characters that surround you. But with this book, you can keep shining the spotlight of your attention on the work of finding out who you really are. So the last chapter is on finding your true self.

Mardi J. Horowitz, M.D.
Distinguished Professor of Psychiatry
University of California, San Francisco
School of Medicine

*Preface*

# Part I
# Identity

# 1
# Roots of Identity

In our lives, we all play many parts. We are an intricate composite, with depths of personality, qualities of character, and a unique, underlying essence. Our identity can provide a sense of who we are over an extended period of time. But at times we may experience a disturbance in our identity or feel depersonalized. And we change. We continuously remake — or even unravel — ourselves from time to time. Beyond consciousness about our identity are unconscious organizations of the self.

Identity is complex. That's no surprise: A sense of identity is only the tip of the iceberg — much remains hidden below the surface and away from view. That's how our subconscious works: We cannot consciously detect what is hidden in the depths of our subconscious mind. Self-understanding uses conscious reflections to bring beliefs and judgments about ourselves to the surface, where we can more easily work with them and better harmonize our values, images, concepts, intentions, goals, and attitudes.

This kind of focus on self-understanding has been called self-reflective awareness, insight, or mindfulness. Quite early in medical school, I heard, "Physician, know thyself." *Knowing* means tuning in to your intuitions, your sense of right and wrong, and especially your motives in whatever you are considering. All these motives, intentions, and expectations rest on a base built in the past — your own past, with years of others defining you, your biology influencing your temperament, your culture representing what your character *ought* to become, and your spirit reflecting who you *want* to become. In other words, we human beings do not start with a blank page. We have a narrative of identity to provide continuity over time, even though our identity slowly changes to reflect our self in each stage of life.

Throughout our lives, we solve problems using consciousness as a tool for constructing a wiser, kinder, and more loving identity. Reflecting involves using our consciousness to view all the facets of ourselves in the long journey into the self, to see the truths and conflicts within our heart and mind. This type of reflection is a learned skill, using self-observation and self-knowledge. We can use this skill to improve our emotional choices — and that is a main focus of this book.

This chapter starts with a look back at the possible past, to get a glimpse of the base from which we can begin again, toward a better future. While reading this book, you hopefully will gain a better understanding of who you are, harmonize your sense of identity, and gain more control over your emotional states. (We emphasize each of these themes individually in the three sections of this book.) A common metaphor for these goals is to see yourself as if you are a charioteer holding the reins of many galloping horses. The central point is that, as the charioteer, you're in the driver's seat: You use your strength and control your own life. To do this, you must find out as much as you can about who you are. This task begins with knowing your roots.

## Defining Your Identity

Implicit in the word *identity* is the concept "over time." For example, I have more or less the same identity today as I did last week. When I go on to say things like "I am identical to myself — that is, I am continuous," those who understand me say, "There goes Mardi (again)." Yes, I continue, but I have different states of self-consciousness for every mood that I feel. I call these *self-states.*

In this sense, I have multiple self-concepts and a conglomeration of perhaps unconscious selves. To put this in terms of the theater, I am always the same actor, but my roles may change. When any one of these roles, or selves, is active, I may experience it as my identity, my sense of who I am now and over time. For example, sometimes when I'm playing tennis, I feel like a great player who can take risks at the net "as always." At other times, I feel "as always" that I am a bumbling, old, and unreliable ball hitter, so I hold back any hard smashes because I am unreliable at this sport. "Mardi the crack shot" is a conscious experience that rests on an enduring but slowly changing self-schematization as *highly skilled.* "Mardi the low-grade player" has an enduring but slowly changing self-schematization as being *so-so in skills.* My self-as-critic deems this unconscious self as more accurate; it emerges from my unconscious and gets its moment in consciousness after I rush the net, smash the ball, and lose the point because the ball went over the fence instead of into the court.

In *An Essay Concerning Human Understanding,* John Locke (1689) called consciousness "the repeated self-identification of oneself." He referred to this self-identification as the responsible agent of conscious thought, emotion, and action. Later, Sigmund Freud (1895) identified unconscious responsibility and got into all the knots implied by consciousness remaining unaware of what unconscious processing is up to. For example, a person may self-flagellate for procrastinating on an important project, while unconsciously feeling dread over actually completing the work and presenting it for the critique of others.

Our potentials for experiencing emotions are unconscious mental structures, and our feelings, our passions, and our traumas are our most intense moments of consciousness. What is not conscious combines with what is outside our self in processing information. It is as if our conscious mind works like the screen in a movie theater: One projector comes from deep inside us, one projector comes from our perception of the external world, and the combined image only partially represents what is real either internally or externally. The screen is consciousness, and we use it to both handle threats and seize opportunity. We discuss these topics more fully at the end of the book. For now, in dealing with conscious identity, we can think of maturity as the ability to moderate our emotions as we deal with those deep internal and massive external stimuli. This doesn't mean that we never allow spontaneous states of love, excitement, and joy. It means that we have a choice to make between embracing the advantages and avoiding the dangers of expressing our feelings. We often make calculations about when, where, how, and even whether we choose to express ourselves — and we have to determine what the consequences of those choices might mean. So while emotional regulation is the topic of the closing chapters, we discuss aspects of it along the way.

## *The Importance of Emotional Regulation*

Our inner thoughts and living environments produce emotional responses within us. Our bodies and minds react to the present stream of stimuli according to primordial influences, acquired attitudes, and situational stimuli. Consciously and unconsciously, we regulate our emotional responses, lest we are flooded with emotions and feel out of control or traumatized. As we increase our capacity to regulate our emotions, we also likely increase our resilience to stress. For example, if we can anticipate an emerging flare of temper and curtail it in the privacy of our own minds, we likely can avoid disruptive arguments in a fragile negotiation with a colleague.

Our identity is strongly affected by how we appraise our capacities and how well we've regulated emotional impulses in recent difficult situations. If we fled from an argument or struggle, we may shame ourselves as cowards. If we flew into a rage with a frustrating companion, we may punish ourselves with guilt and fear what may happen next. We may even anxiously anticipate a threat of searing guilt, overwhelming fear, self-shattering shame, or self-revulsion.

You've surely heard the story of Goldilocks, a child who was lost in the forest until she found refuge in the empty house of the Three Bears. She sat in each of the three chairs, tasted each bowl of porridge, and lay down in each bed. She marked her reaction to each encounter at different points along a spectrum — for example, too hot, too cold, or just right. Mastering our human emotionality means tuning our feelings to attain a "just right" mood whenever we can. Of course, developing skills for better emotional evaluations and judgments takes time.

Too little emotional regulation leads to disruptive thinking and behavior, such as intrusive fantasies or memories, impulsively triggered plans, and appetites that soar into dangerous excesses. Too much emotional regulation leads to inhibitions, avoidance, and an inability to spontaneously go with the flow. "Just right" emotional regulation leads to adaptive boldness and the ability to set and achieve life goals.

We can make significant headway toward more maturity by reflecting on our attitudes and where we may have gotten them. We cannot erase old attitudes from our unconscious mind, but we can counteract and organize them in better ways. Above all, we can intend to keep irrational attitudes from claiming our intentions and plans for action. Let me reword that: We can plan when to think before we act. That, in turn, will improve our self-governance of expressing our emotions. That aim at reconsidering core attitudes is why we start with understanding the roots of self.

The very word *identity* implies an abiding and constant way of thinking about ourselves. But as I have been saying, we are not so constant until we put our internal house in order. For example, many of us implicitly match what we see ourselves doing to an inner framework of how we should behave — an internal set of stage directions, if you will. These sets of beliefs, as in what I *did* and what I *should have done,* often strike a discordant note. A mismatch can give rise to shame or guilt, or perhaps we expect others to notice the mismatch and we fear embarrassment. Sometimes being explicit in our minds about what we expect and what we intend helps us gradually, with repeated effort, change inappropriate attitudes and even excessively harsh self-criticisms or expectations that we will be perfect.

## What Is Identity?

Most people distinguish the border of their identity as their body and its role in society. Inside the skin is me; outside the skin is not me. "One body, one self" is a rule that breaks down quickly when we look inside a mind. In different states of mind, multiple and sometimes confused beliefs about ourselves emerge. You might then ask, "Okay, how do I organize the pieces of myself in a harmonized way?"

This book focuses on the arc between how we currently see ourselves and a potential, somewhat new selfhood in the future. In this chapter, we delve briefly into the past in order to set the stage for understanding how our current self came to be. Chapter 2 continues with ways to observe different self-states. In Chapter 3, we consider the highly important range between a person with a well-organized sense of self and a person whose identity is disturbed by dissociated or disorganized elements, parts, or beliefs.

---

## *Roots*

Our current identity has a unique back story, with roots in our biology and our specific cultural concepts and values. It is also affected by our caregivers and peers during infancy, childhood, and adolescence. Our sense of selfhood develops in emotional relationships with others, whether predictable or erratic, validating or rejecting, nurturing or cruel, and empathic or obtuse. Identity has precursors in genetic allocation and fetal growth, and then emerges in infancy, childhood, adolescence, and adult life.

Much work has been done to understand more about what determines personality and how various factors can lead to the expression or suppression of emotionality, referred to as temperament.

Temperament provides us with certain predispositions that play a role in the development of our emotional appetites and fears. Neurocircuitries and neurochemistry affect our capacity to differentiate internal sensations from external stimuli, understand others, feel others' emotions empathically, copy others, and govern our own emotional urges, needs, and wishes. These biological factors help determine how we seek vitality and learn to tolerate various frustrations and negative emotional arousals. Each of us has traits that include tendencies toward certain moods and types of reactions to the surrounding world. Temperament primarily affects our infant–parent relationship patterns and thus influences attachment by affecting how we perceived care-giving adults when we were very young. The complex strains and joys inherent in this early relationship mold the bonding instinct. Temperament may dictate how easily a particular child is frightened and how quickly he recovers his equilibrium after a fright, or how angry a child gets and whether she is easily soothe.

Culture also shapes an identity and offers instructions on which emotional expressions are acceptable or taboo. Influencing the available routes to accepted roles are instructions on what to learn and how to control urges and feelings. We get these instructions through our peers and the leaders of our group. For instance, certain cultures emphasize individuality and self-reliance (think of the historical West of the United States), whereas others prioritize collective group solidarity over individualization (as in historical Maoist China).

Character is the more socially and psychologically determined aspect of how our emotions are regulated — it's the insider version of reputation. Our minds are formed to function in social groups. We regulate our emotional expressions to gain acceptance and avoid embarrassment, stigmatization, or ostracism. Think back to high school and recall how long you were concerned with gaining respect from others and maintaining your reputation. Reputation is more or less what others think about your character: good, bad, indifferent, trustworthy, interesting, untrustworthy, slippery, tricky, full of integrity, and so on.

Where do adult traits of character come from? They start from infantile emotional interactions and build on what we've been given as temperament.

## Infantile Development

Self-realization begins even before 6 months of age. By 9 months, babies often have the ability to hold the emotional states of others in their minds, likely through recognizing the shades of vocal tones, facial expressions, and bodily movements. A baby who is developing well can talk, referring to him- or herself and others, by 15 to 18 months of age. Babies mimic what they see, and they appear to develop a storehouse of early models for expressing themselves in different situations. For example, a child who observes that smiling elicits tender responses learns to deliberately smile more.

At 7 to 10 months of age, an infant may begin to exhibit stranger anxiety. If an unknown person appears, especially when the baby is not being held in the arms of the caregiver, the baby may show a startled response by staring, exhibiting a fearful facial expression, or crying. The child may also turn to look at the face of a familiar figure, as if looking for emotional cues about how to respond to a stranger. If the parent seems calm, the child's threat response diminishes. If the parent routinely exhibits tension in reaction to these situations, the fear of strangers can endure. (Over time, however, the child can unlearn that attitude. In some cases, learned fear reactions may be adjusted and a measure of reasonable caution is the improved result.)

The degree of security and trust infants feel toward attachment figures affects their later emotional tendencies and adult personality configurations. The categories found useful in predicting a variety of future traits are those of the *securely attached, anxiously attached, ambivalently attached*, and *socially resistant or avoidant* child. The securely attached child may tolerate more "strangeness" in environmental situations and with strangers, as well as short separations from the mother or primary caregiver. The anxiously attached child tends to have less confidence and shows more maternal clinging to maintain a sense of security. The avoidant child has partly given up on the mother as a security-providing figure and is more likely than others to exhibit detachment. The neglected and avoidant child may become precociously mature and appear very self-reliant, but the child may lack the capacity to love or even be empathic to others. A neglected child can also follow many other possible pathways to adult character. For example, instead of developing the ability to cope normally with life's ups and downs, the insecure child may become an adult who is prone to dependency and feels abandoned when a relationship doesn't work out.

The way in which these early categorizations of children might predict later affiliative or avoidant tendencies — including ways in which they are, as adults, able to comfort and care for a baby of their own — suggests that early models of themselves are an important platform upon which later self-organization is built. Babies can carry nonverbal residues of memory and expectations that have been strongly influenced by the effects of their early emotional experience. This may influence all that follows. In cases of neglect or trauma, for example, the effect may change with time. Character can evolve through increased self-understanding and the ability to regulate our emotions.

## Childhood: Developing a Sense of Self through Imitation and Identification

Babies imitate facial expressions and try to duplicate actions, as with this commonly experienced interaction. Observing her mother writing a letter, Nancy tries to imitate her by picking up a pen and scribbling on the table. "Not on the table," her mother admonishes, offering a piece of paper and directing Nancy to keep all the drawing on the paper. In this way, a child learns what kind of imitation elicits positive and negative responses from the parent.

Mimicry encourages action, and repetition leads to an internal model or template of the action. The developments of synaptic pathways in the brain make it easier to perform that action in the future so that it becomes automatic. Sets of such automatic response plans become aspects of a mental model of the self.

Suppose, for example, that a child has a parent who titters nervously when someone else speaks in an angry tone of voice. The child may watch, hear the parent, and mimic the response of tittering; with many repetitions, the child may even acquire this as a habit. Though unaware of the habit, the child may, when yelled at or harshly criticized, begin to automatically titter.

With a constant parental figure, a child may identify with the widespread roles witnessed through family and immediate community interactions. The character of the child may be molded into the character format as interpreted by the child. This involves not only a bit-by-bit assembly by observation and mimicry, but also the adoption of an entire mental model of another person. A child can model a role for self on the activities seen by a parent in that role, as is so often noted in how a child plays with dolls or other toys. The child has empathy for how the parent may be feeling or thinking inside, but it is child empathy (and the capacity for even childlike empathy is lacking in some children). The child may have a self-role as mother, but the role is simplified and "childlike."

Different composite views of selfhood occur and endure in the mind. These represent a variety of possible roles or characteristics for all of us. This repertoire of selves can produce different but recurring states of mind. For convenience, I call these *self-states*. Imagining the game I will play tomorrow or reviewing a memory from last Sunday's match, I may have a self-state as heroic player or I may feel criticized for over-reaching my mediocre skills.

Because there are different unconscious selves, each person has a repertoire of potential self-states and does not remain in any one of them. Identity and identity disturbances may be different in different self-states. Even in old age, we can re-experience a self-state based on a very early in life model of ourselves. In dreams, for example, I can be experiencing my self-images in the unfolding imagined story as a college-age guy with a full head of hair who's seeking a new love, which is quite different from my real self, a somewhat bald, married, older man.

## Childhood Trauma May Strain Identity Development

Children react in a number of ways to early traumatic experiences that put them in a position of extreme and intolerable vulnerability and lead to terror or horror. Traumatic situations with adults or older children bring out their feelings of vulnerability and can contribute to the development of an excessively weak, defective, or degraded mental identity model, along with a greater tendency to feel fear or rage. Parents aren't always able to shield a child from harm. In such cases, some children develop excessively helpless attitudes about themselves by identifying with and imitating a helpless parent. Some children who are abused develop the attitude of victim and, by vicariously identifying with the stronger role, aggressor. Both victim and aggressor role attitudes can impair their much later adult functioning in relationships.

In states of severe protracted and unprotected stress, a child may take in only fragmentary ideas about who he or she is, with no cohesive sense of being a whole, integrated person.

The result can be a state in which the normal sense of self-identity andreality is lost, instead   characterized by feelings of unreality or strangeness. Early traumas may promote later tendencies toward disconnected responses as a personality trait. (However, developing new and healthier responses can lead to resilience, causing the earlier trait to fade over time.)

Faced with vulnerability in a turbulent or threatening situation, a child may focus on the most powerful people in the environment. If these people are aggressors, the child may reverse roles and identify with them in order to align with those who possess the best survival potential. Having made this identification, the child may become a perpetrator and victimize others as an adult because aggression remains the familiar strong role. To justify degrading or harming others, the child victim who has grown into a perpetrator might distort information, for example, by claiming that the new victims somehow deserve the abuse.

Blame is externalized and passed on to a child as a defense against the parent's own potential to feel guilt or shame. A fluid process of internalization and then defensive externalization of fault is involved — the parent takes personal responsibility and then externalizes blame by scolding the child. This can lead to irrational ideas that confuse the child about what rightfully belongs to him and what belongs to others, as when parents project "badness" or fault onto others as a means of protecting themselves from blame.

A related but opposite tactic used to balance identity is idealizing others. A child who, as a result of early trauma, experiences a loss of stability or suffers from a deflated self-image may enter states of mind filled with hopelessness, bitterness, or anxious vigilance. As a defense against these types of feelings, the child may irrationally idealize another person, to derive strength and hope from associating with that person. For example, idolization —

and even mob-minded idealizations — of music or sports stars commonly arise during adolescence as youths develop exaggerated identifications with people they admire. Excessively idealizing some real or fictional person in a child's world holds its own potential for frustration and deflation when the target doesn't perform up to projected expectations. The relationship with the idealized one then feels broken, and all the positive feelings the youth associated with him or her may turn to rage at being let down or abandoned.

Alternatively, a child with a deflated or fractured identity may idealize him- or herself, developing grandiose states of mind to protect against feeling deflated. Ambitions for greatness and illusions of competence can lead to crises when they vastly exceed a person's real potential, skills, and capacities — for example, think of a child wearing a superhero cape who jumps off a roof believing he can fly. Some childhood magical thinking and self-concepts might never be erased. (They are held in check, however, if magical thinking is reappraised with reasoning and emotional governance, as later phases of maturation take place.) Unrealistic ideas may become dormant as the child develops more realistic ideas and uses a kind of reflective self-awareness. I discuss this in detail in later chapters, to help you develop this cognitive skill.

## Adolescence: An Opportunity to Revise Self-Identity

Moving into adolescence, increasing hormones and bodily changes increase sexuality, and turbulent emotional reactions and feelings may arise, along with new and intense urges. When developmental milestones occur during puberty, we revise our ideas about who we are, our internal models of ourselves, and other external dynamics. Other life changes during this time, such as assuming responsibility for the care of younger siblings, also trigger the rethinking and restructuring of our identity; as adolescents, we can generalize from experience better than when we were children.

The brain advances in its synaptic capabilities into adolescence, enhancing its capacity for generalizations about roles and relationships that reflect back on selfhood. That's largely the reason identity is said to crystallize in adolescence. It does not become solid, however, like a crystal. It develops facets like a jewel during typical adolescent experimentation by "trying on" new pieces of identity, much as an actor might try out new types of roles. Important others in an adolescent's life play a critical role by listening and taking the teen seriously, engaging in conversation, and providing a loving and safe environment in which to make mistakes and be loved, no matter what. In the absence of such self-containment, an adolescent is deprived. He or she may turn to cults or precociously like a mature adult — but an adult who is not as open to loving, as might otherwise be the case.

## Significant Endings: Readjusting Identity in Response to Stress

Experiencing catastrophes, extended combat, or major threats and losses calls identity itself into question. The death of a loved one or the end of a significant relationship often signals that it is time to rearrange the personal narrative structure — that is, the story of self that is past, present, and projected into imagined, possible futures. The process of changing from what was to what will be can be marked by sorrow, pining, rage, or a fear of falling apart. Early in the readjustment period, a person may feel as if he or she is deteriorating, but the end result can be an improved sense of self-efficacy and solid identity.

Imagine living through the death of a beloved partner. Soon after the loss, you are still attuned to the whereabouts and structure of life with your partner: When is she coming home? Where is she going to sit for dinner? What will she wear? Discovering through experience that the other person is not just away for a short time, but is gone forever, is one step toward revising your ideas about who you are.

A survivor's identity and mental repertoire of relationship models change as he or she comes to terms with being a single person who lives alone, makes decisions alone, and, at some point, potentially seeks a new partner. Mastering such challenges to identity can lead to a sense of greater resilience, competency, and coherence within a growingly conscious answer to the question, "Who am I?"

Personality traits such as a tendency to avoid taking responsibility for actions that have a bad outcome or that cause you to feel incapable of making new and good choices can lead to problems in revising and then understanding a sense of self after a crisis. For example, Bob had an insecure attachment to his mother and went through several difficult relationships before marrying a woman who provided him with an abiding sense of security in their intimacy. He functioned much better during the marriage than he had before, even at his place of employment. His wife's positive reflections and emotional support made him a better person. He felt in control.

Then his wife died. Bob lost a vital relationship that had helped control his insecurity. He developed social phobias and suffered from states of extreme panic, depression, and sorrow. With time, patience, and effort, Bob learned ways to tolerate the loss. As a temporary aid, he relied on a partial replacement relationship with a helping figure — in his case, a supportive and empathic psychotherapist. He learned to be alone without panic, as well as how to connect with another person who could give him the kind of emotional containment his wife and then, temporarily, his therapist provided.

## Relationship Experiences Help Improve a Sense of Identity

Most of us need the company of others to feel and be our best and to develop a strong sense of identity. We approach life not as a one-man show, but as a production filled with a sometimes large cast of supporting characters. We are social creatures with emotional needs for relationships and positive connections to others. It is difficult to survive, much less thrive, in isolation. Companionship is a critical part of how we view ourselves, even when experience has made us shy and distrustful of others. People undergoing crises may learn the skills they need to bolster their own identity through identifying with others.

If you share your problems and dilemmas by confiding in a friend or a therapist, you can observe how your confidante handles the situation. You might depreciate the helper by saying, "You're not doing anything to help me; you're not tough enough to handle this — you're just worthless!" However, even in a state of anger and frustration, you watch the helper's reaction carefully and remain aware that the helper does not become demoralized, lose self-esteem, or abandon you. From this experience, you can identify with the stamina of the helper and learn by example how to hold up in the face of criticism and threats to yourself, while still maintaining a strong sense of identity.

People who have traumatic experiences in childhood may or may not carry vestiges of the trauma with them into adulthood. Some may retain and harbor a plan for repair or revenge after an experience of abuse or neglect. These plans can be revived when current relationship situations echo the childhood experience. For instance, an adult may respond with childish feelings of magical hopefulness for a more satisfying joining in true love. If these hopes are dashed, a plan for revenge might emerge. Change comes with reappraisal of all these lingering motives, recognition of the actual reality of the current situation, and an understanding of the way it differs from the childhood situation. Careful thinking leads to rational formulation of a plan of realistic actions and appropriate self-restraints.

## *Points to Remember*

- Identity is rooted in development. A sense of continuity over time characterizes identity. That means self-organization is complex: It has to both endure and change slowly. That change is a life narrative about self, and vast aspects of that narrative are not conscious.

- To resolve identity conflicts, having discussions with a confidante or writing personal journal entries helps put problems into words. This can lead to modified beliefs about identity and result in a clearer life plan.

# 2
# *Self-States*

Most of us feel and act differently, and even seem to have different values, when we're in different states of mind. In other words, we're the same principal actors, but we're acting out different characters in the theater of our mind. We are the same but different, and we notice these variations in attitude. Someone close to us may also pick up on them, perhaps noticing fluctuations in *our* moods more than in their own.

Who has not said, "You're not yourself today" or "I'm not myself today"? We often make these kinds of comments when our emotions feel or look a bit out of control. For example, when we're intoxicated, we're operating in a hazy state — we're "not ourselves." Likewise, when we suffer a hangover, we can't shake off the feeling with a cup of coffee. But instead of resting our focus on occasional states of mind, we're better served to pay close attention to recurrent and undesirable patterns. For example, drinking alcohol may activate a change in attitude from caring to belligerent, or from prudent to reckless. In some recurrent states, a person may accuse or mistreat others and then, shifting into another state, become remorseful and again compassionate and kind.

Usually we're dealing with less extreme states than those riddled with dejection and self-degradation. In fact, noticing a subtle established pattern of emotional expression or inhibition can be challenging. We are so familiar with ourselves that we may not get clear signals about our shifts in moods. It may take engaged effort and honest reflection to recognize a pattern that we want to modify. Naming typical and multiple self-states is a first step to gaining more insight and, thus, more self-control.

One helpful method is to reflect upon yourself, considering how well you are regulating your tapestry of feelings during any particular state of mind. For example, suppose you have hostile feelings toward someone you're with. You might reflect on a time when you demonstrated what you were feeling — in this case, angry belligerence and a sense of being a bit out of control. Perhaps you noticed that the other person even seemed to worry about whether you were fully in control. At that time, you weren't following the same emotional script as your companion. At another time, in a different state of mind, you might have been more in control, assertively presenting your anger and expressing yourself as you intended. You didn't get overly aggressive because the situation didn't call for it. Your actions matched the emotional script that society and you expected. Then in yet another state of mind, you might have disguised your internal irritation by assuming an air of carefully imposed politeness. An alert observer might have sensed what was beneath this mask and intuitively known what you were stifling, but most people are not such alert observers. The script, in this case, took center stage and masked the real character underneath. In these different states, you are projecting your feelings outward in ways that can, for the purposes of discussion, be called over-, under-, and well-modulated emotions.

## How to Reflect on Self-States

Listening to your inner self means expanding your field of awareness to observe experiences at the edges of your inward, conscious mind. At any given moment, you can notice a multitude of thoughts, ideas, sensations, changing moods, and intuitions. Actors do something similar when researching the people they are portraying so that they can more easily step into their characters' shoes. When you make time to reflect on your own flow of consciousness, you can ask some insight-provoking questions:

1. Are you expressing your thoughts and emotions clearly or in an indirect manner?
2. Is a sense of concealment working at the fringes of consciousness?
3. Are you frequently in a state of doubt because you have contradictory ideas? Is an idea expressed and then retracted?

Yes, these questions are difficult to answer at first. Do not let that dismay you. By taking just the first step and asking about your inner experiences, you will notice an improvement in your ability to pay attention to what is going on. When you can, pay attention to your degree of emotional self-control as you change from one attitudinal state to another. You can use general categories as you look at and identify your emotional regulation: well-modulated, overmodulated, and undermodulated.

## Well-Modulated States

In a well-modulated state, we exhibit good self-management and seem at ease with our feelings, even negative emotions such as boredom or fear. Our responses to others are generally spontaneous and open, even when we are irritated, and our words and accompanying actions feel harmonious.

For example, one of my patients, a middle-age man, was having problems with his business partner. He needed the partner's financial advice but found dealings with him prickly and unpleasant. The patient described the way he managed the conflict and expressed his own feelings of frustration and anger. As he did so, his emotions were clear. His irritation clearly came through in his speech, gestures, vocal tone, and facial expressions. His manner signaled that he knew I was listening and understanding his feelings, and that's what he wanted. He was in a well-modulated, working state.

## Overmodulated States

In an overmodulated state, a shield of self-concealment arises between others and our self. If we are in an intimate conversation, we may reduce eye contact, choose our words more carefully, and veil our inner thoughts. Spotting such signs isn't difficult. When the man who spoke frankly of his anger at his coworker later began to speak of his frustration with his wife, his direct and clear tone changed. His eyes narrowed, his speech took on a muted quality, and it was more difficult for me to inquire about his feelings toward her.

## Undermodulated States

In an undermodulated state, a person's usual degree of self-governance and control goes out the window; impulsiveness takes over. While observing such states in my clients I hear outbursts of excessive exuberance, harsh anger, or embarrassed sobbing. I see jumpiness, jitters, grimaces, giggles, or gulps. When the same client who had just been so guarded when focusing on his marriage suddenly shifted his state of mind from overmodulated to undermodulated, he let loose a volley of emotions about his rage and sorrow. During this explosive display, he seemed completely unaware of my presence for a few moments. Undermodulated states are the most uncomfortable states for ourselves and others, which is one reason most of us go to great lengths to avoid them.

## State Transitions

Paying attention enables you to note when you shift your degree of emotional control or sense of identity. At this point, I add shimmering state to your categories for self-observation. This state contains antithetical elements and may have both over- and undermodulated aspects. Characteristics can include uneven emotional inflections in voice, halts in speech, wandering attention, incomplete ideas, a tendency to shy away from or retract already-expressed ideas, a vaguely jittery feeling, and rapidly reversing beliefs or values. For instance, the patient who was so vexed with his wife in an undermodulated state told me, while in an overmodulated state, that he felt he had gotten used to their disagreements and we didn't need to discuss them further. I asked him whether this was actually so. He repeated that we could drop the topic, but then he entered a shimmering state: His eyes filled with tears and his fingers nervously plucked stitches from the arms of the office chair where he was seated.

Let me repeat this important point: By trying to notice the play of emotional ideas in your present mind, you are not merely gaining insights into your attitudes; you are also improving your skills at paying attention. This builds your capacity to observe yourself. As that happens, you get a bird's-eye view by recognizing and naming your own personal states of mind, beyond the general "modulation" categories I've discussed.

## Jim's States of Mind

Jim, an intelligent 35-year-old business executive, displayed a limited range of expression and control of his emotions. When he first came to see me, he reported a lack of motivation in his work and social life, along with a general withdrawal from the world. He came to therapy when he felt worried about the security of his job. He had high monthly expenses and significant credit card debt, and he could not afford to be out of work.

Jim worried that he would soon be fired, which seemed to me like a real possibility. Upon my inquiry, Jim pinpointed the start of his downward spiral at work as the period immediately following his promotion. He had developed an innovative approach to marketing his company's products and had been rewarded with a raise and an increase in responsibility. Jim's new duties included supervising a handful of staff and delivering periodic reports on the progress of his unit to management. Jim would get enraged when people he supervised didn't meet his expectations or when he felt criticized by his manager. We agreed that it would be useful for him to be able to pay attention to his feelings of anger.

Jim recognized episodes of hostile explosions. These undermodulated outbursts appalled and embarrassed him. His manager had directed him to attend anger-management classes. Because Jim didn't know how to change his response patterns, his solution was to avoid any situation that might lead to an outburst. He isolated himself from his colleagues as much as possible, withdrawing into a self-protective shell. Together we drew up a list of the various ways he felt angry. Then we looked at the list to see how he managed his anger in different situations, from the mildest annoyance and irritation to his tyrannical storms of irrepressible rage.

The most maladaptive and undermodulated state for Jim was *blind rage*. In this frame of mind, he wanted to demolish whomever he was confronting. If someone was frustrating him, destructive impulses were all that filled his head. In those moments, he lost awareness that his rage was a storm of emotions that would soon abate. If he had ever liked this person, he could not recall it. He couldn't imagine ever liking this person again. In this moment, during this state, the person at whom his anger was directed was cast in his mind as a nemesis and archenemy. Jim's realization that a change-of-state buildup was taking place did not surface to clear consciousness until he paid attention to his own state transitions and differences between states.

A second, shimmering state of mind for Jim was one that he labeled *blurted-out irritation*. Different from his blind rage state, in this frame of mind, he didn't want to obliterate an adversary, but he was not in full self-control, either. He didn't care if he left a wake of hurt feelings behind. For example, when I was a few minutes late to let him into my office, he muttered, as if to himself, "Typical tardy professor! He couldn't care less about me!" In the session, he quickly retracted his statements and apologized for being irritated and speaking rashly.

In contrast to these two states, Jim also had a state of anger that he modulated successfully and called in the privacy of his mind *appropriate irritation.* In some instances of mild annoyance, such as when he saw that a colleague had misspelled his name, he had a direct and capable response. His sharpness remained under control. He asserted himself appropriately, spoke to the issue, maintained respect for whomever he was confronting, and smoothly moved past the inciting topic. Jim also had an additional state of anger that seemed overmodulated, and as I drew attention to those qualities as a recurrent pattern, he named this his *sullen, grudging state.* In this state, he shut down, backed off, and pouted. For example, when denied a position on a committee, he became withdrawn and silent for far too long during the meeting. He initially believed his impassiveness protected him from exploding and cloaked his inner reality from others. In time, however, he came to realize that others perceived this state as a negative coldness that veiled some other complaint.

In his sullen, grudging state, Jim suppressed his irritation by exerting enormous effort in speaking carefully. When in this state with me, he spoke in a slow, surly monotone. Soon he could recognize his entry into this state and find his own way out of it. As Jim's attention to his various states of mind continued, he came to learn that his sullen, grudging state was uncomfortable for others.

Jim was a bright man. On an intellectual level, he certainly understood that emotions cannot be amputated from the human experience. But unconscious attitudes have an inner psychological reality beyond logic or rational thought. When we began to put Jim's semiconscious and not particularly verbal attitudes into words, we began to observe a shimmering state of mind. During this state, Jim began to talk about how his manager was to blame for some recent flare-up; then he halted his speech and, apparently, also his private thoughts. He took back the last phrase and said something even more critical of himself than his manager would have been. He went back and forth, and I could observe in Jim the signs summarized earlier on shimmering states.

The attitude that often led into these states was a desire to "find someone else to blame" for some matter that had not gone well. Shimmering emotions included anger at the other for blaming him, but Jim's states of mind were complex. Not only did he criticize the other person, but the other person was also criticizing him. The shimmering emotions, then, were anger *plus* embarrassment. Soon Jim and I realized that self-judgments were part of his underlying concern. This led us to examine his potential for feeling shame, which is where we uncovered additional significant attitudes.

Unconsciously, Jim preferred feeling anger over shame. To protect himself from feelings of shame, he became angry or, depending on the circumstances, exhibited other protective emotional states. For example, sometimes he put up his shield and withdrew. For Jim, shame was much more distressing than anger, so his not-so-unconscious mental processes efficiently protected him from feeling that shame. To avoid blame and feelings of mortification, Jim became enraged and blamed others. Being angry and getting lost in a blind rage helped Jim feel strong — even if only temporarily: He could blame others instead of feeling embarrassed. Rage permitted him to steer clear of the "weaker," more vulnerable state of shameful mortification.Paradoxically, his undermodulated temper outbursts were a source of potential shame.

Yet another state of mind that Jim liked to experience repeatedly arose when he presented his innovative marketing idea to his colleagues: He was rewarded with praise, a raise, and a promotion. Jim and I called this frame of mind *exhibitionist excitement.* Naturally, this state is a pleasurable place to be for most of us because we tend to enjoy both admiration and a boost to our self-esteem. However, in his new position, Jim was compelled to present his work regularly. In some instances, he was rewarded with further exhibitionist excitement; alternatively, if his presentation fell short and was questioned or criticized, he experienced shame.

Jim had a wish–fear dilemma. He wanted the excitement and pleasure associated with presenting his creative ideas. However, presenting them was scary because they might fall embarrassingly short of some standard. When we have a wish–fear dilemma like that, we get tense and even anxious, which may unleash our inhibitions, avoidances, or escape mechanisms.

When anticipated risk is great, our unconscious mental processes ward off a dreaded state by maintaining a protective or defensive stance. In doing so, however, we also sacrifice the possibility of achieving the desired state. Nevertheless, emotions cannot always be controlled or neatly curtailed; other moods continue to emerge.

Unwanted urges and wishes can leak out and make for messy, confusing, and uncomfortable moments.

Jim's dilemma created anxious anticipation for him, which led him to withdraw into his office and enter a defensive state that he and I named *ruminative rehearsal*. In this frame of mind, Jim went over what he would be showing his colleagues without really feeling ready to present. Checking his plans gave him a sense of strength and reassurance that he was reducing the potential for embarrassment. Unfortunately, this ruminative rehearsal contributed to excessive procrastination, which created more discomfort and anxiety, leading to greater potential for embarrassment.

Labeling states like *ruminative rehearsal* helped Jim learn a new kind of reflective awareness. He began to see patterns and gradually learned to stop himself before he entered an undermodulated state such as blind rage. Recognizing his self-attitudes was the beginning. Later Jim discovered more about his various self-concepts and ways in which he expected both great success and great failure. Above all, Jim learned how to become more self-aware and gained more authority as his own chief agent, governing the way he expressed his feelings.

As in Jim's study of self-understanding, you are beginning a process of what will become a gradual increase in understanding yourself. Different states of mind show that you have different attitudes — even about who you are — in different frames of experience. Your deeper attitudes do not come quickly to the surface: You must wait for them. As you do so, you can begin noticing and reflecting on how you think and feel in your familiar but different states of mind.

## *Conscious Self-Awareness*

Now let's consider an exercise in self-state examination. Recall being in a certain state of mind. Examine and re-examine every aspect of the memory. How intense were your feelings? Did you feel the same way other times? How far back can you recall feeling that way? Did any important person in your life have similar states of mind to those you are now confronting?

Monitor your assessment of your experiences over the last week or so, using a rating scale for just this purpose. Table 2.1 helps you rate the degree to which you are experiencing generally desirable "positive" states. You can even photocopy Table 2.1 and continue to monitor yourself over time, to see if you are gaining in satisfaction.

**Table 2.1:** *Positive States of Mind Scale (PSOMS) (Horowitz, Adler, Kegeles, 1988)*

**Instructions:** Label and fill in your state of mind. Circle 0 to 3 for each type of experience in the last seven days.

| State of Mind | Unable to Have It | Trouble Having It | Limited in Having It | Have It Well |
|---|---|---|---|---|
| **Focused Attention:** Feeling able to work on a task you want or need to do, without many distractions from within yourself | 0 | 1 | 2 | 3 |
| **Productivity:** Feeling of flow and satisfaction without severe frustrations, perhaps while doing something new to solve problems or to express yourself creatively | 0 | 1 | 2 | 3 |
| **Responsible Caretaking:** Feeling that you are doing what you should do to take care of yourself or someone else in a way that helps meet life's necessities | 0 | 1 | 2 | 3 |
| **Restful Repose:** Feeling relaxed, without distractions or excessive tension, without difficulty in stopping it when you want to | 0 | 1 | 2 | 3 |

| **Sensuous Pleasure:** Being able to enjoy bodily senses, enjoyable intellectual activity, and activities you ordinarily like, such as listening to music, enjoying the outdoors, lounging in a hot bath, kissing, caressing, or having intercourse | 0 | 1 | 2 | 3 |
|---|---|---|---|---|
| **Sharing:** Being able to commune with others in an empathic, close way, perhaps with a feeling of joint purposes or values | 0 | 1 | 2 | 3 |

After you assess your positive states of mind, you will probably find that some are rated as not up to the level of "have it well." This may be temporary due to some pressure, stress, or crunch on you. However, if that is not clearly the case, you may need to work to gain more satisfactions. You may want to sort out your goals and possibilities, considering where you rated low. Most psychological self-help books start with this important principle, but it is not always easy, quick, or reasonable. Showing persistence and adopting a dose-by-dose attitude can help you accomplish this hard task of knowing what you want in relation to what you might obtain from your life, and making plans to achieve possible self-states.

---

## *Points to Remember*

- Labeling states of mind with words gives you a small but valuable increment of control over your emotions and your particular attitudes within a state. By considering the amount of control you may be feeling or displaying in any emotional state, you can decide where you need to monitor yourself more.

- You can identify the states of mind you want to have more frequently or with longer duration. Similarly, you can examine the opposite end of your spectrum and name the states you want to avoid entering or have only briefly.

- Paying attention to shimmering states makes it easier for you to identify topics that are restless or unresolved within your own mind. The shimmering may occur partly because you have multiple attitudes that are not yet well harmonized. In every chapter that follows, we discuss the advantage to calmly expanding your thinking time so that you can put these attitudes into words, compare and contrast them, and revise your appraisals of what is most important to you.

# 3
# Coherence

The journey toward a harmonious and integrated identity isn't easy. To some extent, our journey toward a harmonious self recalls the "hero's quest" pattern of many epic movies. The main character, generally a youth, faces trials and tribulations in a quest to save the world — or at least his own world. In the same way, we face the task of a lifetime in consolidating our sense of identity. We begin as adolescents, struggling to figure out who we are, how we fit in with others, and what we want from life. We continue to wrestle with these questions, and more, as young adults and into adulthood.

The ancient Greek philosopher Plato defined the task of building our character as finding ways to integrate our intellect, our spiritual values, and our appetites (usually for pleasure or the satisfactions of wielding power). Freud later defined these three parts, or a "braid" of ourselves, as ego (intellect), superego (morality over the "I" of ego), and id (the it-like function of biological drives). Pretty much all philosophies, Eastern and Western, and all psychologies have struggled with the idea of the self having parts — often even parts in conflict — that maturity and wisdom can better blend.

Our language for conversations and self-reflective awareness focuses on social functions, not on issues such as identity. So let me define a few words I use throughout this book. *Self* refers to the entity that we are — that is, a bodily self containing a brain and mind. *Identity* refers to a reflection about this entity, the self. Identity has a sense of continuity over time — for example, I am the same self today that I was a week ago. Self is a thing; identity is a thing thinking about itself.

Identity brings a problem: For harmony, it needs continuity and constancy, but it also must deal with constant change and the process of changing. Because identity endures while yet slowly changing — for example, as we age and acquire new responsibilities — identity is a sense that can be disturbed. In fact, people are more aware of disturbances in a sense of identity than they are aware of their identity when their beliefs about self are reasonably consolidated and balanced.

Identity disturbances are common, as in these examples:

- Adolescents are notorious for their struggle to consolidate a sense of identity that provides self-respect.

- Multiple-personality stories command a wide audience because we identify, to a degree, with the characters represented.

- In clinical depressions, deflations of identity reach irrational degrees of self-criticism. A person may feel or express, "I am a totally worthless person."

- In psychotic states, concepts of self and other are transiently but frighteningly confused.

- After a traumatic event, many people experience depersonalization. That is, they go on being aware of perceptions, but they feel unreal, without their usual intuitive sense of having a continuous identity from past to present.

- When a loved one dies or divorce occurs, people must rebuild their sense of identity even as they grieve their loss.

Identity disturbances are not just an either/or state of having a coherent identity or having identity fragmentation due to a crisis of self-reflection. We do not have unitary self-beliefs. We each have a repertoire of multiple self-schematizations — unconscious belief systems of who we are — operating within our overall identity. Finding a way for our various self-schematizations to work together in harmony supports a sense of who we are over time. Our aim is a coherent identity, but we get there by working on our identity-disturbing thoughts, feelings, and behavioral patterns.

A sense of identity consistency is called *coherence*. Naturally, some of us have more of a sense of coherence than others. For emotionally healthy young people, the work of establishing an inner coherence of identity may have progressed quite satisfactorily by the time they complete their education and are ready to step out into the world to begin a career, find a partner, and perhaps start a family. Most of us would probably say that we encounter many young adults who are "solid and full" inside. But as therapists know, this is true only up to a point — and it is often mostly in appearance.

## John's Path to Normal Maturation

John was lonely in high school. After graduation, he joined the military. He served for eight years but decided not to re-enlist. Instead, he entered college on an educational plan funded by the government for veterans. Even though he was immersed in his class work, he yearned for an intimate relationship. As he sought to meet women, he noticed his sense of self-confidence slowly declining. Sometimes he shifted into states in which he felt like an inept teenager.

Like anyone else, John liked to present himself to prospective dates as a desirable man. His manner reflected how he wished to see himself: as a strong, intelligent, and amusing companion. He knew some women would find these traits attractive, but John's view of himself sometimes changed and he appeared to be incompetent and uninteresting. For example, at parties, when his ideal self-concept dominated, he projected a *vivacious and excited* state of mind. When the inept view of himself reigned, however, he acted *timid and tentative.*

At a friend's party, John looked across the room and noticed Sue, a pretty woman he had never met. As he introduced himself, Sue showed signs of interest. They sensed each other's excitement, made plans to see each other, and began dating regularly soon afterward.

After some time, John and Sue no longer presented their best behavior to each other. Sue discovered that John's attitude shifted; he seemed awkward, secretive, and quiet. He misunderstood her, especially when he was feeling morose. After moments of sexual intimacy, John seemed tense and withdrawn.

Sue was disconcerted by John's shifting styles of being himself. John observed that Sue's moods could also change. Sometimes she felt and acted like a damaged child; other times, she complained that "too much was expected" of her and "too little was given." He was surprised to learn that Sue had different self-states as well.

Their relationship became dull. To regain a sense of vitality in his life, John broke it off with Sue and turned to another woman, Jane. As with Sue, courtship with Jane was exciting at first. The new relationship caused him to feel the rush he desired, and he again presented his charismatic side. John felt some remorse about the way he had abruptly ended his relationship with Sue, but he remarked to his friends that she must have been bad for him because, with Jane, he was happy again.

Once the novelty of the relationship with Jane wore off, though, John fell into his same pattern. Sometimes he thought Jane had changed. Other times, he felt he was repeating an unhappy script. Frequently, his mood shifted and he felt inept, dejected, lonely, and hopeless. His pessimism was exacerbated by periods of heavy drinking, during which he experienced episodic emotional storms and bitterly lashed out at people who seemed to have satisfying relationships. John felt extreme despair at his own dismal loneliness and began to have suicidal thoughts.

The repetition of intrusive ideas that his life was hopeless and might as well end was not connected with any plans to actually hurt himself. But John did recognize that this could be a mood he had to address. He realized he was startled by his pessimism and began to examine his own sense of who he was, now. His prospects for the future were not dismal, but he did not have the closeness and loving relationship he craved. He sought help from others he trusted and began a process of self-reflection that led to significant changes in his outlook, as well as significant changes in his behaviors with others.

John adopted a more steady and enduring view of himself and also discovered that he felt better as a reliable member of a couple. He stopped blaming his partners for his own loss of interest in intimacy. This development involved changing his values. His goal of sexual excitement for momentary thrill became a low priority; he assigned a higher priority to a new value of shared closeness over extended periods of time.

He still liked Sue, and after he explained and apologized, she agreed to resume their relationship. John worked on himself instead of blaming Sue for his sour attitudes. He paid attention to the important fact that Sue had supported him through his up-and-down moods. He tried to support her when she was irritable or distant, and she noticed it. When one of them had an "off" mood, John and Sue stopped seeing the other as a "bad" person and stopped interpreting it as a reflection on themselves or their relationship. They learned to enjoy the moments they were attracted to each other. During times of stress, when one or both felt bad, ugly, or incompetent, they developed empathy for each other. Their increase in mutual understanding helped them both feel more consistently whole and worthy. John then came to feel that he was a good and strong person because he was able to help Sue though periods when she was down instead of leaving her.

John's maturation in his relationship with Sue illustrates how an individual with several self states can, over time, bring them into greater harmony.

## *Identity Disturbances*

We have an unconscious self-organization. We have a usually intuitive sense of identity: We are the same from past to present, even though we have matured, aged, and experienced change events. But sometimes our unconscious self-organization is threatened. Then we may consciously have a sense of disturbed identity. Depersonalization, or dissociation during traumatic events, is one example of how a threat can move us beyond a latent sense of identity coherence to a more conscious sense of identity disturbance.

People with frequent disturbances in their inner sense of consistency may unconsciously split appraisals of themselves into all-good and all-bad clusters. Splitting concepts makes it difficult to hold two or three nuanced thoughts simultaneously in conscious reflections of what is happening, perhaps in a relationship under strain. Believing "I am good" or, at other times, "I am bad" can lead to segregation instead of coherence. In these instances, we fail to recognize that we can have conflicting beliefs. In other words, we must avoid the types of archetypes that we often see onscreen or on stage, as in the moustache-twirling villain or the angelic blue-eyed blonde. A more complex and appropriate understanding would be "Sometimes I'm good and sometimes I'm bad." Likewise, viewing ourselves as part of a "we" in a marriage or family unit can lead to an all-good or all-bad characterization.

Relationships may challenge our sense of identity, especially if the most significant other person in our life feels very controlling or very rejecting. The other person may change moods or behaviors toward us. Even satisfying attachments will experience periods in which they are frustrating connections. Likewise, normal changes in someone else's mood may contribute to a sense that the person has shifted from being benign and caring to the opposite. When our ability to conceptualize is unstable, we can experience abrupt changes, from relationship bliss to relationship hell. In such a case, a typical response is to try to influence the other person and alter our self-presentations to stabilize a relationship.

Inauthentic presentations of our self to others can seem like an act, and the act may fail to fully satisfy anyone in the long run. British psychoanalyst D. W. Winnicott developed a hypothesis about a "false self." The person with a false self is like an actor who capably enacts a social role of the external self as poised and secure. In reality, however, that person is inwardly experiencing a state of emptiness and inauthenticity. Deep reflection can make the self seem like an imposter. Winnicott theorized that a false self can result from a failure to cope with and resolve highly disturbing experiences in early childhood.

Children cannot observe or realistically process strong emotional reactions to trauma because their mental apparatus is still so immature. A traumatized child operating at this level might believe that the abuse heaped on him is not to be questioned and is therefore deserved. He then may form an enduring sense that this submissive false self is realistic, that others believe it, and that he truly has bad qualities inside him. In such a case, a split takes place between a "good self" and a "bad self," likely resulting in a disturbed self-organization.

Matters can worsen if parental figures fail to offer a genuine and attuned reflection of the child's actual good nature. British psychoanalyst Melanie Klein hypothesized that when a child sees negative feelings such as envy or anger coming from the mothering figure, the result can be a kind of primitive paranoia. That is, the parent may change moods from one that gives the child security to one that threatens the child. The child wonders who is to blame for the change. An early response is a kind of irrational rage: *That person is out to frustrate, hurt me, or abandon me.* Klein calls this a paranoid position on who intended what to happen. A later, equally irrational, response might be what Klein calls a depressive position: *I am to blame for all this distress. I only do wrong. The situation is so sad, but I do not know how to make the future any better.* Anna Freud, Sigmund's daughter, became a psychoanalyst and continued her father's emphasis on the child's sexual and aggressive drives in triangles of drama called the Oedipus Complex (the triangle of mother, father, and child — sibling rivalry can be added for the core early psychoanalytic model).

In the middle of theoretical arguments about what is most developmentally important in constructing self-organization is John Bowlby, who emphasized the primacy of a search for security in a trusted attachment as a way of preventing terror. In this theory, attachments of security protect the growing self-organization of a child, and abuse or neglect impairs coherent development of the self structures that unconsciously support a conscious sense of identity. From the earliest age, infants search for closeness to a trusted adult, usually the mother, to soothe and protect them from possible threats. Even as adults, we reach out for more security by attaching ourselves to others when in dangerous or strange situations.

Across the channel, French psychoanalyst Jacques Lacan emphasized the early incomplete, dependent, and helpless qualities of infants. When they feel negative feelings such as fear, they view themselves as being vulnerable. Young children learn whether others are threats or safe figures. Secure attachments help the young develop a firm sense of selfhood because the trusted other reflects back to the child what the child is like and emphasizes that the child is worthy of attention.

American psychoanalyst Heinz Kohut took this a step further by examining empathic attunement over time, first between baby and caretaker and then between child and parent. He identified a partial self–other fusion that, through mutual caring and reflectance, led the child to form self-definitions and coherences at an unconscious level. Interestingly, not only did the child use a parenting figure as a self-object, but the consistent care-giver also used the child as a self-object. Both gained identity, satisfaction, and even pride from attachment to the other. Kohut contrasted this growth with narcissistic vulnerability. In such a case, the parental figure might use the child as just an extension of herself or might not empathically tune in to and reflect back the real character of the emerging individual within the child. As a result, the child might emerge into adulthood vulnerable to identity disturbances.

American psychoanalysts Daniel Stern and Robert Emde hypothesized that infants learn self–other models that are unconscious structures about social relationships. These models are affected by culture and genetics of temperament. The unconscious attitudes of infancy and childhood lay down a structure that, if not modified in latter developments of a narrative structure of one's total self, can lead to a variety of self-states. These may lead any adult to a range from realistic to unrealistic self-judgments. A conscious sense of self-esteem and identity coherence can be disturbed by unconscious self-criticisms and unjustified attitudes. To mature, adults may need to repair their early ideas about who they are.

## *Varied Self-States*

In different states, we have different levels of identity coherence. I oversimplify this conceptualization with the categorical listing in Table 3.1. Categories listed refer to the present moment and adult states of selfhood.

**Table 3.1:** Self-States

| Level | Description |
| --- | --- |
| **Harmonious self-states** | When in these states, an intuitive sense of self is unified. When experiencing conflicts and negative moods, internal conflicts are appraised as "of the self." Realistic pros and cons are examined to reach choices of rational action and restraint. In these states, people view others as separate people with their own intentions, expectations, and emotional reactions. In conscious representations, perspectives on relationships approximate social realities of the present moment. |
| **Mildly conflicted self-states** | An intuitive sense of mild identity disturbance may occur when a mismatch arises between personal roles and roles the outside world seems to expect. Mild identity disturbance can also occur when we have incompatible personal goals. An inability to choose a single goal leads to a sense of discord, as in whether to approach or avoid some kind of relationship. Irrational views of a relationship also may stand in the way of caring attachments to others. |

| | |
|---|---|
| **Vulnerable self-states** | Identity may seem to shift between intense divergent emotions. Illusions about grand personal traits may defend against self-disgust, fear of failure, or a strong potential for shame and self-degradation. Rage may erupt at others who are perceived as insulting. In such states, people may use others as tools of self or may externalize blame onto others. |
| **Disturbed self-states** | People organize their mental life using self-schemas that do not match reality. The self may be confused with others in terms of who did or felt what. Rage may be seen as stemming from others. Within the self, thoughts may be confused with memories. Fantasy may be confused with completions or real actions. |
| **Fragmented self-states** | A massive chaos of identity can occur. People may believe the self and other are merged. Parts of the body may be disowned. Poorly regulated suicidal or homicidal urges may emerge because the threat to identity is intolerable. |

## Clarifying Self-Attributions

Increasing harmony by listening more carefully to our intuitive sense of who we are is a lifelong task, but many techniques can help. One such technique is clarification, which involves using words to make ideas clear for us so that we can address our own personal goals and values. Putting our values into semantic form teaches us how we tend to automatically and nonverbally judge ourselves. This may sound obvious, but it's not necessarily so clear. We tend to experience ourselves as agents — that is, "It is I who am experiencing this stream of perceptions, imaginations, and bodily sensations." Putting that into words is not ordinary. It often adds cause-and-effect reasoning. For example, "My stomach has butterflies" states a sensation. "My stomach got butterflies right after I was told to present my work to the chief" begins to put one thing with another.

Goals and values are what life coaches and therapists of all brands tell you to put into words so you can reflect upon them. That reflection helps you clarify reality from fantasy. It also is a way of defining who you were, who you are, and who you are planning to become: your continuity, but also a slow change in identity.

As you put your values and goals into words, you may find beliefs that contradict reality. For example, a woman with light brown skin may have internalized the value her elders passed on to her that "lighter is better" or that "darker is better." Along the way, a good teacher might have shared the belief that it is wrong to judge a person by skin color. And as a child, she might have been told to embrace opposite viewpoints and to reject contradictory alternatives. The woman is in a triple bind! If, as an adult woman, she can be clear about all three points of view and see where the various beliefs come from, she can sort out the concepts and make her own choices to reach a new, explicit value. She might realize that she has nice skin and approve of herself, while, at the same time, recognizing that the history of her elders and teachers led to their various views. She can agree to disagree with the voices that seem to echo old restrictions in her present mind.

## *Reorganizing Self-Judgments*

Values are sometimes personified. That is, you can experience an order to "shape up" as if it came from a critic inside your mind. Some people experience this as if someone else, such as a parental or judgmental figure, were speaking to them. Of course, that is how we were socialized: Our actions were praised, attended with interest, curtailed, reprimanded, or even ignored when we wanted response. We were shaped. As adults, we can do more self-shaping.

It is good to realize that these inner critics are a part of self-organization, even if the critics were modeled on a parent who created the rules and frequently uttered commands to obey them. In the theater of your mind, several critics may be sitting around a table arguing while you're on stage. Now is the time to become the chairperson of this kind of moral discussion within your own mind.

When you encounter what seems like an unrealistic, harsh, self-judging attitude, you need to clarify its meaning. Ask yourself where it came from. Then, in a calm state of mind, challenge its relevance to the present reality of your life. You may then develop a more reasonable belief and an accompanying behavior. If so, repeat this process often.

You're probably thinking, "Sure, but it's much easier for you to say this in a book than for someone to do it in reality!" You're right, but by enacting the positive value and repeating it over time, you almost certainly will reduce excessive self-criticism and moderate a few blows to your self-esteem.

How do you know your efforts at increasing harmony are working? Here are some signposts to watch for along the way that indicate your work on self-understanding is progressing:

- By reducing the harshness of some inner critics, you begin to acknowledge your limitations more accurately, but without being as harsh on yourself as before. Perfectionism is inhuman and inhumane.

- You gain a bit of pride and self-confidence because you have accepted the responsibility to improve your self-judgment.

- You regard outside pressures not only as stressors, but also as challenges to prompt you to develop more self-efficacy.

- People who know you show more respect for your composure and constancy.

- You choose more reasonable goals than before and persist in developing the skills to attain them.

- You develop an innovative solution for your persisting and difficult relationship problems.

- You experience states of mind in which you feel real and grounded more of the time.

- You can appreciate the accomplishments of others as well as your own.

In short, we all have a tendency to foster different self-states. This list defines some ways to harmonize them. The kind of relationships we have, and our present attachments to others, give us the courage to make this effort and to find ourselves in the eyes of others — and that is the central topic of the next three chapters.

## *Points to Remember*

- Don't be surprised to find that you experience a kind of repertoire of self-states — that is, states of mind that occur repeatedly but change your sense of identity during them.

- You can sort out self-states by naming them in your own way, which helps you consider your motivation to change. Which ones work well and which ones would you like to experience less?

- Pay attention to the kind of situations that precipitate self-states you do not like to experience. Just naming these observations will start to give you more self-control.

# Part II
# Relationships

# 4
# Unconscious Connections between Self and Others

For most of us, relationships are central to our pursuit of happiness. We prefer to experience life as a character-rich production than as a soliloquy. Those connections to ourselves, family, friends, work mates, and the world greatly influence our contentment and our self-states. These affiliations tend to endure — and slowly change as memories we have generalized from our past relationships. We use these generalizations or schematizations as a kind of map for now and the near future. These cognitive maps have inherent emotional potentials, and they are important in grounding our intentions and expectations. Some of these maps impair our opportunities to make the best, most realistic decisions. If so, they qualify for revision because, without change, we cannot fully take advantage of real opportunities for closeness and caring.

From time to time, even in loving relationships, painful and confusing events occur. We remember these as potential future threats to our well-being, to help protect ourselves in the future. In other words, our memories help us decide how to proceed and how to avoid distressing or even catastrophic situations. We must update our unconscious models of relationships so that they do not limit our identity growth or inhibit us from intimacy or effective cooperation with others.

We all have unique internal maps that develop from the fundamental biology of our brains and also what we learn from experiences. These experiences change the brain itself, through neuroplasticity. We continue to learn throughout our lives, but we base our lessons on the past, as our foundation for how we interpret the world and ourselves.

In earlier chapters, I mentioned that our self-concepts are largely unconscious, unless we experience threats to self-organization. In those cases, we may experience quite consciously disturbances in our identity, such as depersonalization or discord between self-states. We then become more conscious of other people, trying to figure out what attachments and affiliations are safe and trustworthy, which are threatened, and which may be risky or even exploitative. This makes up a set of stage directions for us, or templates of self and others as interacting in various potential ways. These guides organize us during the moments we are interacting with others and the world. This is why, in a play of inner motives and outside pressures, we tend to automatically replay our same old patterns. Others see our personality as these patterns.

Consider being a parent, for example. We focus on our child and how to care responsibly and with warmth. But we can also contemplate our own role, especially when we note that we are or were in a state of mind that was not compassionate or kind: We think about our self-states in the relationship and, in the process, may uncover unconscious self-conceptualizations and expectations about what parenthood brings us. We may have irrational expectations: "My child will, in every state of mind, be totally loving toward me." Of course, such expectations can only lead to unhappiness.

There's no shortcut to shedding old patterns, but we have much to gain by observing those habits and making changes for a more harmonious outlook, both within ourselves and in our relationships.

## A Mother, a Daughter, and a Grandmother

Alice's daughter Loni had her first child by Caesarean section. Loni was exhausted and invited her mother to come and help with her newborn daughter. Alice was excited and pleased by the invitation and arrived while Loni was still in the hospital. She busied herself cleaning Loni's house and prepared a convenient place where the baby could be diapered and bathed. While preparing what she named the "diaper station," Alice was especially pleased as she imagined Loni smiling with gratitude when she saw such a sweet space prepared for her and her new infant.

Loni's reaction was quite different. When she saw the diaper station, Loni spoke irritably to her mother, saying that she had planned to set it up differently. Alice experienced a sharp change in mood. She felt stung and hurt by Loni's criticism, and her demeanor turned cold. She pouted, struggling to keep herself from acting on her impulse to storm out of the house.

Alice had expected Loni to admire the diaper station and respond enthusiastically, as she had when, as a young girl, she had received a new present from her mother. Alice misunderstood her new role as a grandmother. She was still playing the role of a competent and admired mother, the center of Loni's attention. That relationship model hit a serious discordant note when Loni spoke irritably about her own, independent plans for the diaper station. Still drawing on her past script, Alice reacted as a hard-working mother providing help to an ungrateful and selfish daughter who did not appropriately respect her authority and productivity. So, as in the past, Alice concluded, "Loni expects me to do only menial services, such as the laundry." Alice felt justified in angrily expressing her hurt feelings. She felt indignant that, instead, Loni expected *her* to express remorse. After all, Loni had disrespected her as a mother.

After thinking it over for a time, Alice realized that she needed a new attitude. When she carefully reviewed her own feelings, she realized that she was clinging to an outgrown model. Though it didn't feel normal at first, Alice eventually came to see herself as a competent grandmother offering care to her tired daughter. Over the next couple weeks, when Loni expressed irritation, Alice paid attention in a new way and made a conscious effort to let go of her antiquated attitude. She surprised herself by soothing Loni and supporting what she wanted: her own individual role as a competent mother. By adopting a new attitude, Alice was able to respond gently to Loni's irritation instead of with indignation and sullen behavior. The result was better not only for their mother-daughter relationship, but also for Alice's sense of herself as a coherent, harmonized person.

As in Alice and Loni's case, any new relationship is contextualized and understood in terms of our past experiences and what we have learned from them. Previous relationships persisting as models of ourselves-related-to-others can complicate our views, and past fantasies or bad experiences can set the stage for future unpleasant experiences.

## *A Scientific Perspective*

Neuroscience has identified the most complex aspects of our internal modeling of relationships. The complicated prefrontal cortex of the brain is invested in performing this interpretative task successfully. The prefrontal cortex connects by tracts to many other modules of the brain. Information goes in and out, and generalized cognitive maps of social information are retained and modified. These circuits compose a kind of master map made up of a series of individual maps, any of which might guide our actions or expectations in a particular situation. These models provide us with a repertoire of potential attitudes, but they are not clearly accessible in our conscious minds. Worse yet, damage to this area of the brain can limit a person's capacity to develop and use appropriate ideas about themselves and others. As a result, accurate perceptions of other people's intentions are less available, and empathy becomes quite limited.

Scientists have located "mirror neurons" elsewhere in the brain. To learn how to best understand another person, such cell networks and tracts have to function well. Tracts connect areas of the brain such as the insular cortex, mirror neurons, and prefrontal lobes, and it takes the whole network of brain regions to truly process how we relate to ourselves and others. Assuming that these brain areas are reasonably well functioning, most of us are capable of improving our abilities to understand ourselves and others, and can learn new attitudes. A repeated, careful, and conscious effort to do so can improve intimacy and help establish a set of shared rules that serve as a foundation for building the trust and fidelity necessary for a long-lasting relationship.

The key to such improvements is conscious reflection on the question "What is happening in and between us?" In other words, understanding what is actually taking place often means considering wishes, desires, intentions, motives, and enduring attitudes — in other words, our expectations. An actual interpersonal relationship can contain new elements. Noting these properties can change old attitudes. This process of learning can be impaired by persistent use of outgrown models of self and others that first developed in childhood. You can ask yourself questions to help identify what is realistic now and how that differs from what has happened in the past:

- What do I hope will happen?

- What is the difference between what I need and what I desire?

- What is this person's intention toward me and our relationship?

- What does this person need, and how might that be different from what he or she desires?

- Who is afraid of what? People often talk about what they like and dislike, but conceal their deeper fears. Thinking over big threats can make some ghosts vanish or lead us to realistically prepare for something.

These questions help make conscious what is unconscious so that we can reasonably contemplate it. As you continue to ask yourself these questions over time, your new answers may not be the same as the ones based on earlier ingrained attitudes.

## *Making Changes by Revising Attitudes*

Change would be a lot easier if the only issues we faced came purely from our current life situation, but it isn't that simple. Most of us grow up in a family structure of some kind, a framework of past experiences. When we model our behavior on past relationships and how we related to ourselves and others within an old system, we often let our past set the stage for our future experiences.

### Understanding Frequent, Problematic Attitudes from Childhood

Many common childhood attitudes cause discord when we replay the old patterns in our now-adult situations and relationships. All sorts of childhood experiences can lead to problematic attitudes that persist fairly unnoticed into adult life. Looking to the past is often helpful in guiding your choices in the future. Gaining a general understanding of how closeness with others develops may help clarify how your prior experiences shaped your perceptions and attitudes toward trusted associations, and can aid you in revising your patterns for interacting (with yourself and others).

Children suffer if they feel unloved, regardless of the circumstances. Even if caregivers are unable to show love because of illness or impoverished circumstances, children may blame them. This childhood sense of injustice and dissatisfaction can persist and develop through adulthood, into either an expectation of compensation or a desire for revenge. In fact, some of us have a vague sense of guilt because of our revenge fantasies for grievances, as if thoughts are magical and can produce destructive consequences. Superstition about curses stems from these fantasies.

A child sometimes turns his response inward and develops the mindset that he has not been loved because he is, at the core, "unlovable." This degraded image may influence thoughts such as, "I will never be loved — I am weak, dirty, and defective." To undo this prophecy, the child develops heroic plans, such as to win the Nobel Prize by discovering a cure for cancer. This plan becomes an obsession to prove that he is finally worthy of love.

Other times, children stop short of their best effort and fail to achieve their ambitions. For example, a girl who takes up the violin as a child may subconsciously think, "My dad is proud of how well I'm learning to play the violin. But he plays the oboe even better than I play the violin. I want to grow up to play the violin even better than he plays the oboe. No, that's dangerous. If I were to play better than he does, he might feel envious of me. That might hurt him, so I will not try very hard; I will stop short of excellence."

From this chain of thought, a life pattern can develop of stopping short of our best effort and failing to achieve our ambitions. This can hinder good relationships with mentors and colleagues, and damage self-esteem. Another version of this dysfunctional attitude is, "I will do my very best," but then unconsciously continuing the thought with, "and I will find some way to punish myself in order to make it up to my father."

Taking the thought even further, upon succeeding as adults, we might unconsciously throw away new opportunities afforded by hard-earned success or become depressed rather than satisfied with the fruit of our achievements. A corrective change in attitude might involve recognizing that people both compete and cooperate, and we need not feel traitorous in succeeding or feel ashamed if someone else does better. Instead, we can learn to appreciate our own and others' skills and accomplishments. We can adopt a new attitude by realizing that we would like to be the very best and resolving to try our hardest. But if we do not come out on top, we can accept the fact that another person earned the top honor.

## Learning New Attitudes about Intimacy

Overcoming a limited or unhappy approach to relationships often means revising attitudes learned during childhood and can involve more than one relationship model, as is the case with Andre.

Andre's behavior with women was often based on multiple scenarios that used old relationship models.

**Relationship model #1:** According to his chivalric, romantic model, Andre was a good, heroic, and spiritually devoted person who admired physically abstinent or "asexual" women. He was platonically "in love."

**Relationship model #2:** Another model he had of himself was as a lusty stud who took advantage of a woman unable to resist his sexual advances. He would seduce her into committing erotic acts she would otherwise refuse to be involved with on moral grounds.

**Relationship model #3:** Andre also had a role–relationship model that involved a powerful, dominating woman who could cast a spell on him, eventually smothering and trapping him.

In the beginning of a relationship, Andre would approach a woman with gallant courtesies, thinking of her according to his romantic love model. In his fantasies, he would rescue her from a predatory person, such as an abusive boyfriend, and she would admire and adore him. Then the scenario would shift and she would morph from the desirable and devoted woman into a domineering and demanding woman who might trap him in a marriage he did not want.

According to this attitude, made up of three relationship models, Andre expected some women to control and use him. His self-concept changed from the role of rescuer to that of victim. His fear of some women stemmed from his view of them as spiders who snared men in their web.

Andre was able to correct his attitudes by gradually being more open to new experiences and by forming a more adaptive, flexible observation of how the women in his life actually behaved. He learned to observe that they felt sexual, self-controlled, and equal to him rather than either subordinate or superior in virtue. His irrational attitudes changed slowly, resulting from his new determination to carefully observe and reflect while participating in his day-to-day life. Encouraged by his success, Andree learned more realistic views and broadened his understanding of the complex roles women and men can take with each other in different states of mind. Eventually, he was able to overcome his limited approach to relationships and had a realistic chance to establish a committed relationship.

As mentioned, a good way to learn new relationship patterns is to reappraise what is really happening. We can listen and open ourselves to consider what can happen next. This open, receptive stance involves wondering about the other person's mental intentions, not just what is said. In doing so, it is wise to know that all family members, close friends, and intimate partners have multiple stored attitudes at their disposal for forming a current working mental model of the relationship. Established or old patterns organize perception, interpretation, and appraisals in different states of calm, excitement, or frustration. Some attitudes usually remain dormant in a present-moment situation. However, we can unconsciously interpret a present-moment interpersonal situation according to several role–relationship models occurring at once. This is known as parallel processing and is discussed in Part III, "Processing Emotional Meanings."

The main point here is that each role–relationship model in a personal repertoire of attitudes can be applied to better understand what might be going on in an immediate or impending situation. Each model elicits a different interpretation of the situation, which, in turn, produces different emotional responses. These script like patterns do not achieve full consciousness, but may emerge as premonitions; we may experience the aroused emotions without fully knowing why. For instance, you may suddenly clench your stomach when a current experience unconsciously triggers a disgusting association from the past.

## Adam: Parallel Processing of Social Interactions

A fuller example of parallel processing with role–relationship models is provided in the case of Adam, a graduate student in physics. Adam was long overdue in getting his doctorate because he kept procrastinating in writing his thesis. He consulted periodically with the professor supervising his thesis, yet he often delayed status reports of his work. Procrastination jeopardized his career, and he sought help from a psychotherapist to get past the dangerous pattern of avoiding potential advancement in his work.

During discussions with his psychotherapist, Adam got help in clarifying what was going on in his mind about his relationship with his own work and with his graduate-school supervisor. Four different relationship models governed his maladaptive behavior. In the first state, a working state, Adam's role–relationship model with his supervisor was one of mutual positive regard, both given and received. Unfortunately, unconscious triggers, either from within or based on his perceptions of his supervisor, sometimes caused Adam to organize his experiences according to other role–relationship models. For example, if the professor seemed impatient and abrupt, Adam shifted to his state of ruminative worry. In this model, he viewed himself as an incompetent pupil or child interacting with a harshly critical authority figure. The scripts of each role–

relationship model began the same way — with Adam exposing his problems — but in this alternative and negative scenario, he expected the authority figure to label his shortcomings in such a scornful way that Adam would feel like giving up his work.

Most of the time, Adam was in either a working state or a state of ruminative worry. The more he delayed, the more he worried. However, two other states occasionally emerged. One was a state of excited fantasy, in which he imagined that he was a great scientist illuminating a problem for his professor. Adam fantasized that he could solve an important scientific problem that his professor could not, catapulting himself to fame.

The last role–relationship model prominent in Adam's theme of procrastination produced a state in which he viewed himself as a complainant. He would annoy others with a kind of whining attitude. In this state, he depended on his teacher to do the necessary intellectual work for him. The teacher would not do all that Adam expected, no matter how much helpful interaction was offered. If and when Adam recognized his attitudinal behavior, he felt disgusted with himself for a combination of inappropriate ingratitude and dependency.

Adam's repertoire included four self-images contained in the four role–relationship models: sincere student in the working state, incompetent child in the worried state, great scientist in the excited fantasy state, and needy, deprived child in the whining state.

By paying explicit and repeated attention to the difference between his old established attitudes and the reality of the student–professor and patient–clinician situations, Adam became capable of having franker, safer experiences of negotiation. He stabilized himself in his working state and developed a more competent and coherent view of his career growth possibilities.

Fostering more adult views of yourself in a relationship may help you reorganize your thinking while you are in a reasonable and calm state of mind. However, childlike views have not been erased from your mind and might take over your thinking in stressful situations. Under stress, you might regress from the sophisticated adult models to childhood attitudes. As soon as you can, strive to restore a state of calm, in which you can use reasoning to again progress to using mature organizing views of yourself and others.

## Tools for You to Use

Tools are available to help you progress beyond repeating ingrained attitudes to exploring what you want — that is, creating new, realistic patterns. For true intimacy, you want to feel authentic and grounded in a way that increases kindness, trust, and commitment. Your best tool is consciousness: being aware of your own patterns of thinking and their consequences in the moment, acknowledging your feelings but also keeping your emotions in check so that you may engage in reasoned contemplation.

The first step is to use tools that help you recognize that what is happening is not optimal. This recognition might be intuitive, or you might feel that you are "stuck in a rut." Second, you must look for one of your problematic states and give that state a name — a label that helps you reflect on your state of mind (perhaps "sulking"). We discussed this already in Chapter 2, "Self-States." Then clarify what does not work when you find yourself in this state. For example, you might ask yourself if you feel out of control in your emotions or in the way you communicate them to others.

The third step is asking yourself what you like about this state. That is, what purpose might sulking serve for you, even if you do not like the negative attitudes it may contain? Your response might be something like, "I like feeling justified, and acting petulant corroborates my sense of grievance and dissatisfaction with the world I have to live in."

Here's the point: Even negative, unwanted states of mind often serve some purpose. They may ward off even worse states of mind. For example, sulking tells another person that you feel unfairly treated because you are not getting the attention you feel you deserve. It can elicit attention, so it is preferable to despairing, which feels even worse. Having evaluated the underlying emotions, you can put an attitude into words, such as, "When I sulk, I want you to respond by first apologizing and then giving me what I want." Putting attitudes into self-talk helps you reassess the rationality and/or effectiveness of a particular stance.

The fourth step is to ask yourself why this apology or reparation is so important — namely, because it can get you out of the problematic, unwanted state (sulking, in our example) and keep you out of the dreaded state (that is, feeling neglected and abandoned).

Once we can put our intentions and expectations into words, we can use reflective awareness to review their real usefulness or maladaptive purpose. We can reason toward better ways of relating to ourselves and others. Instead of sulking to get a response, we can talk about our feelings and negotiate as adults, perhaps modifying our desires and offering a give-and-take proposition. You can start this reasoning by talking to yourself, asking a question like "Is what I want and expect likely to occur? If so, how do I encourage it to happen?" You may come up with an answer such as, "I feel frustrated that this person neglected me, but I hope he will come around and be more available and caring. To encourage this, I plan to be kinder, more attentive, and more compassionate toward him. I'll let him know what I need, without complaining or being too demanding." If that outcome seems unlikely, the answer might be something like, "I feel frustrated because I know this person has other concerns, so I will not get the attention and response I want right now." In the second scenario, the hope for healthier attention seems unrealistic. In that situation, how can you correct the unrealistic expectation and get over your mood of disappointment and resentment?

When the chances of getting what you want are slim, here are some suggestions for possible changes that might improve your capacity to cope more effectively:

**Learn new attitudes**. "I am not going to get the attention I want from this person, but that does not mean I am a worthless or lost person (as I have tended to believe), or that this person is always going to be selfish, unjust, or incapable of changing his behavior toward me."

**Do something positive for yourself.** "I am going to do something I enjoy that makes me feel good about myself and stop sulking, being preoccupied with self-pity, and worrying about the frustrating memory of how I was neglected."

**Do something positive for someone else.**
Another satisfying option in this situation is
doing for someone else what you had wanted
done for yourself. It is both a way of establishing
a connection with someone and an act that makes
you feel empowered rather than neglected or
powerless. This is role reversal with a positive
twist. Helping others, without neglecting your
needs, leads to respect and pride in yourself.

Conversations, questions, improved communication,
and a willingness to negotiate can lead to more successful
interpersonal relationships. When you use tactful and
repetitive questioning, gently prodding for clarification,
you can help others resolve contradictory attitudes and
emotional discord. You can do this for yourself by taking
on a role as your own best friend.

Change requires that you compare distorted views with
more reasonable appraisals. Of course, if your view seems
nagging and critical, the other person (or even yourself in
response to self-criticism) may feel insulted and resentful
rather than helped. As you progressively feel more clear
and secure, you will find that you can examine previously
unthinkable topics. For example, optimism about possible
fulfillment of what you really desire can powerfully
counteract tense and anxious moods. For example, if you
are afraid of asking an acquaintance to a movie, you can
role-play what it might be like to do so, or even what a
coffee-break conversation with your friend might sound
like.

## *Points to Remember*

- For most people, relationships are central to the pursuit of happiness.

- Inner wishes and outer pressures influence which role–relationship models are activated from a person's repertoire. Relationship disruptions are repeated when outdated models are activated and then produce ingrained points of view.

- A person challenged by a new situation may observe it closely and construct a new working model. Reflection can teach ways to improve future actions.

- More adaptive attitudes require careful self-monitoring for a time; then, because they produce positive results, the new attitudes can become new habits.

# 5
# Yourself in Relation to Others: Changing Unrealistic Beliefs

Just like actors expanding their scope, we need patience and a small amount of daring to try out new approaches to our work and social relationships. Our ingrained patterns are familiar, and we seem to often follow their script unconsciously. When the pattern is not in our future best interest, however, we can try to change it. At first, change can feel awkward and strangely new, but with repetition, we can choose a more adaptive pattern in place of an unrealistic one. We need to choose, plan, and act if we want to change old patterns into healthier ones.

In an earlier day, psychotherapists believed that change meant recognizing a recurrent maladaptive or counterproductive interpersonal relationship pattern, tracing its roots to childhood events and stories, and interpreting the motives behind why it was unconsciously repeated. Now psychotherapists know that the major improvements in social functioning and self-comprehension come from acquiring new conceptual skills and, above all, practicing improved ways of experiencing and acting within a relationship. The older view isn't wrong — change simply requires changing. This means taking the time to work on it, checking out new opportunities, making new decisions, and practicing new approaches. Part of the task may involve becoming more aware of shadows of the past that have too much influence over how we behave in the present. This kind of amplified awareness can involve checking up on our beliefs by putting them into clear words so we recognize where characters from our past may be over influencing our present attitudes.

## Taking the First Steps

Our present outlook, self-state, motivations, emotions, and governing values come from unconscious information processing, which is the way our complex brain networks and connections became organized from birth to the present. The resulting internal effects on how we feel and act can sometimes seem more like residues of long-ago experiences than attempts to seize new opportunities for pursuing happiness or reducing our fears for the future. To correct erroneous expectations, we need to make old attitudes explicit. If we can learn how to declare them to ourselves clearly, we can form clear and counteractive concepts.

This self-comprehension process starts with efforts to use self-awareness in reflective consciousness as a powerful tool for knowing, with clarity, what we are feeling. After we take the first step, we can often reach more clarity by asking ourselves what we remember from when we previously felt the same way. Suppose that I feel hatred for a frustrating, selfish, and too demanding acquaintance. The anger can emerge as an overall feeling that translates into body language, like a clenching of fists and a gnashing to teeth. I need to first regulate the feeling — think but not act. Then I can translate the feeling of hating a person into words: "I want to shout at him because he withholds his attention from me." Those words clarify the "why" question, which is what triggered my anger. By thinking further, I can ask why, in the here and now, the attention was withheld — why I felt not just ignored for a moment, but also totally rejected, causing the irritation to descend into hatred. Of course, "why" questions lead to other, deeper issues, such as "Why was his withholding attention so distressing to me?"

Experiencing rejection and speculating about why I felt the other person was rejecting me can be clearly explained: "He withheld his attention from me because he despises me as a worthless thing!" Paraphrasing explicitly clarifies the burst of feeling. In this case, hatred is now an attitude that can be challenged and contrasted with more realistic views. The distress was more intense partly because of the concept "I am a worthless thing," as if I needed his attention to feel like a worthwhile person entitled to live a caring life.

Once we can state an attitude that seems discordant to our current real life, we can reconsider the attitude. In this example, I can reconsider my hatred for a rival who has undermined me in a way I perceived as unjustified, unfair, and hurtful. I first need to reappraise the current situation — is it as I thought it was? I have to appraise in my mind the intentions of this other person. In the privacy of my mind, I can rehearse a potential interaction that might make me more effective in the future. For example, suppose I need to reach some level of cooperation with that rival to preserve equanimity in our work place. I plan in advance to check my irritation at the stage door. I will not say you were unfair and I want to retaliate by criticizing your past work and actions. When I am on stage for our interaction I plan a dialogue on the topic of the near future, on how we can agree on ground rules for how we will be debating the relative merits and needs for material support in the management conference that is coming up in the next scene. I even plan my tone of voice: firm, accepting, unsarcasatic, uncorrosive, and as amiable as can be.

When I repeat this plan, I can see if I get positive feedback. I can assess if my rival means that feedback, and can be trusted, or otherwise. When we carefully notice rewarding results and highlight the positive consequences of new behaviors, we help ourselves firmly establish new patterns. With time and practice, we can become more adept in our new ways. Healthy adult habits will replace maladaptive ones.

## Early Attachments to Parental Figures and Lingering Residue into Adult Life

A parent can function as an envelope of safety around an infant. The infant cries, the caregiver responds. The way in which needs and responses are repeated results in a role–relationship model of attunement and comfort. When care is provided that is consistent with and adequate for the needs of a particular child, that child is usually able to develop character traits of optimism that can sustain him through periods of strain.

Inconsistency, deprivation, or traumatic lapses in care result in an insecure attachment. The child may even develop persistent character traits of pessimism and mistrust. Such enduring attitudes tend to increase the likelihood of worried, tense, anxious, and depressed states of mind as an adult, even though the person may not be aware of the roots of these unwanted moods.

At the other extreme, imagine parents devoting themselves so fully to a baby that they give of themselves instantly the moment anything is needed. The child may, as a result, gradually develop a self-schema of being adored and perfect, entitled to receive unwavering care and admiration from a slave-like worshipper even when he behaves badly. In such a case, the child may display a sullen, demanding, or hostile attitude. Once the child begins to interact with others beyond the home, he may sustain what amounts to some damage in overall self-conceptualization and to knowledge of having secure attachments of others. To prevent damage to his self-esteem, the child may hatch fantasies of greatness, of being a superhero or child of royalty misplaced into the present home. Repeating such reassuring fantasies to protect against the shakiness of feeling vulnerable and too alone, the child may stick to grandiose self-views and unrealistically amplify attitudes of entitlement. With any ill feelings or unfortunate events, others will be blamed, with feelings of resentment. As an adult, these depictions can lead to narcissistic personality traits which may be unconscious and are better called narcissistic vulnerabilities. Of course, life is complex, and in addition to narcissistic vulnerability, some children are treated to a role as prince or princess for perhaps too long or too much, as in the case of Morgan.

## Morgan: An Unrealistic Demand to Be a Star

Morgan's childhood was dominated by an ever-present and constantly doting mother. His resulting self-centered sense of being special did not gradually decline, as it does for most cherished infants in later childhood and adolescence. Instead, Morgan maintained the illusion of his near-godlike status. As his worldview expanded, he learned in school that other children were older, brighter, stronger, and more competent that he. Admitting that he was not always the center of admiring attention made him feel too vulnerable, so he unrealistically demanded that everyone see him as a star. To bolster this star self-concept, he used his large weekly allowance to purchase gifts for friends. However, those friends merely took advantage of him because, in spite of the bribes, he was arrogant and abrasive. When Morgan finally began to look at himself, he recognized these alienating traits. He was unconsciously expecting his mother's admiring cocoon to continue to surround him.

---

## *Overcoming Patterns Originating from a Childhood of Neglect or Traumatization*

Perhaps the most common and unrealistic interpersonal patterns stem from situations in which a child is abused for extended periods or not given enough parental attention. These situations can result in continuing feelings of vulnerability into adulthood. Some adult-dependent personality traits can also result, partly from clinging to an unreliable and occasionally hated caregiver as a young person. Over time, the child comes to expect the caregiver to shift unpredictably toward or away from a responsibly nurturing role. As a protective response, the child must disconnect any feeling of anger. The child demonstrates a facade of only being loving and deserving, hoping that this display will evoke a nurturing response.

If a child has experienced loss or lengthy, repeated separations, she may develop a self-schema of an abandoned waif pining for a neglectful caregiver, whom the child sees as hopelessly gone and refusing to return. In this sad state, the child may try to elicit care from others, yet that experience may make her feel shameful. Consequently, the role–relationship model may be one of an embittered self, looking with hostility upon a world of unfair people and envying those with desired traits. Depression and withdrawn personality traits may remain into adulthood.

The repetitive and maladaptive interpersonal patterns that arise from such enduring attitudes undermine chances for intimacy. The resulting lack of closeness to others impairs adult self-organization because states of loneliness, sorrow, and despair creep in and destroy any hope of maintaining desired connections. That is why personal efforts at self-understanding should aim resolutely, patiently, and repetitively at modifying this pattern.

Expectations of neglect and abuse are most likely to develop when caretakers are depressed, alcoholic, addicted to drugs, or distracted by severe social, economic, or wartime strains. This scenario can also result if caretakers were abused or neglected as children. In these situations, the child may resort to desperate behaviors to elicit better care giving and the provision of food, shelter, and emotional care. For example, parents whose interests in care giving are flagging may be revived into showing concern and care if their child falls ill or is injured. If this happens often and the response is satisfying to the child, she may learns that script: In the future, when her deep need for care is frustrated, she may unconsciously choose to experience and exhibit suffering in order to receive care. In this case, the caregiver contributes to a seemingly masochistic or self-injuring trait. Suffering first becomes a necessary prelude to care; later in life, it can become a more calculated means of satisfying a need for more attention.

Sometimes in adult life, another person is cast into the role of a "bad" parental figure in a drama staged in the theater of the mind. Another character is viewed as a rescuer and supplier of care. As the drama unfolds, we provoke the bad, neglectful caregiver and seek rescue from that person in a theatrical display of neediness or injury. Books that study personality term this reaction histrionic, or overly dramatic.

The display of neediness can also lead to what is sometimes called a *passive-aggressive* personality pattern. This occurs when a person acts needy in order to provoke another to take responsibility for providing care. The person may at first receive care with a show of gratitude, but a latent attitude of resentment, anger, and expectation that care will not be well provided is also commonly present. The person then tries to prove that the caregiver is neglectful, intrusive, or incapable of providing the right kind of care. This form of self-justification of hatred is actually self-defeating.

## Chet: A Passive-Aggressive Pattern

Chet, an administrative assistant to a top executive, was asked to work with another executive whose administrative assistant was on vacation. He resented leaving friends in his previous office, an irritation that was heightened when the alternate executive demanded high-quality work. Whenever her instructions were not explicit, Chet carried them out incompletely or with slight errors. Even if her instructions were clear and explicit, Chet did his assignment very slowly and without interest. If he was not given exact instructions about what to do after completing a task, he remained idle instead of taking on other obvious tasks.

The executive became increasingly irritated and finally lost her temper during one of these episodes. Chet had used the interdepartmental green stationery for an important outside letter that Chet knew should have done on white letterhead. In the explosion that followed, the executive cursed Chet. He, in turn, acted as though he was extremely hurt by what she said. Chet complained widely and threatened to file a harassment grievance, saying that he had been harshly castigated for a trivial error and that she had given him poor supervision. Feeling threatened by a possible human resources review of a complaint against her, the executive became scrupulously courteous to him, tolerating for a while his poor performance and his sullen demeanor, while documenting his errors and productivity level. Chet's passive aggression continued to hinder him: He was often sullen, and other people remained ambivalent about him, blocking the possibility of his promotion.

Pressed by a good friend to confront his possible loss of employment, Chet learned to use his mind more acutely. He realized that he could do better than to go on repeating this pattern. He examined the memory of what had happened in exchanges with the executive. He revised a plan for how he might handle the situation in the future, and he rehearsed how to speak about his frustrations in a way that was both assertive and respectful. His bitterness cooled, as did his fear of being fired. He felt proud that he was learning higher work skills and could get ahead.

As selfless and polite as society may tell us to be, we all crave recognition and attention. Few of us get all the respect, love, and friendship that we want all the time, in every way. The way we handle this discrepancy is a vital aspect of our personality. Some people seek power and control to overcome the gap between what they want and what they get socially. Others pretend to be less effective than they could be, in order to become dependent on others to guide them.

Both the narcissistic personality trait and the dependent trait are a search for attention. Rivalry for attention can lead to jealousy. At an extreme, a wish to get rid of a rival may also make us feel like an evildoer. If so, there is usually a childhood root in unrealistic expectations and in an exaggerated view of competition as being harmful. For example, we may hold an early view that when one needy child gets attention, the other needy child or the parental figure is diminished or undermined. When this belief prevails, we may resent another person for expressing a desire for attention and need for care.

Instead of understanding that love grows between people and that mutual kindness and care giving improve emotional support for all parties, people with lingering rivalry issues may regard life as if it were a zero-sum game that only one person can win and may even fear loving, lest it impoverish them.

## Passivity

Instead of exploring the world with energy and enthusiasm, the child becomes very passive and obedient. All actions conform to what the parent wants, in order to avoid feeling the threat of abandonment. The situation may seem quiet, nonturbulent, and devoid of interpersonal conflicts, but the very safety of this compromised role–relationship model can set up the child for a lifetime of limited identity advancement.

If the pattern is not remedied, in adulthood, the child may behave with a pervasive fear of separations and have difficulty in behaving boldly, creatively, or adventurously. Others affected by this pattern are able to provide guidance and assume responsibility, but mutuality and spontaneous sparks are dulled. A way to build personal social skills and counteract these passive personality traits can be to learn how to be more assertive. You can learn to disagree diplomatically and still be your own person, looking out in an enlightened way for your own best interests.

## Aggressive Acting Out

Another child may handle a fear of abandonment quite differently. Instead of keeping to a docile role, he may choose to identify with a parent's apparent self-centeredness. If the parent handles stress by selfishly abusing recreational drugs or alcohol, engaging in promiscuous sex, or chain smoking, the child may see any of those behaviors as adaptive, strong, self-protecting responses to a frustrating situation. The child imitates the perceived "strong" parental role instead of feeling "weak." Although it may seem strange to describe abusing recreational drugs and alcohol as a way of strength, a child may see it as a positive, forceful move at filling personal needs and identify with the activity. The person has an illusion of self-sufficiency by using various props but has not developed true self-sufficiency.

## Struggling for Power

In response to the instructions of a parent, a child may want to comply in order to gain attention and praise. At the same time, the child may want to act without restraint and have power over self, others, and objects. The child learns that, although parents can punish and reward, they, too, can be made miserable and, therefore, by manipulation, can be controlled. Habits that persist into adulthood, especially in relationships, are developed in this type of childhood testing ground.

Parents, of course, developed into who they are as a result of their own childhoods and cultures. They developed their attitudes in the context of their relationship with their own parents. As we have discussed, role–relationship models can be reversed. As these people become parents themselves, their child–parent role–relationship models are reactivated, but this time they are occupying the parental role. This reactivation of the familiar child–parent pattern is common no matter how much a person disliked the treatment received as a child. In repeating history, we can deeply dislike the tendencies now manifested in ourselves that we disliked in our parents, as was the case with Sharon and her three-year-old daughter, Annie.

## The Power Struggle between Sharon and Annie

One day, Annie was standing on a stool while her mother, Sharon, was arranging pages in a loose-leaf notebook at a counter. The little girl imitated her mother, putting pages together — but not in order. Sharon asked her to stop, saying, "Mommy will be done soon. Just wait a minute." When Annie persisted, Sharon repeated her remark more firmly. Annie ignored her mother and kept on sorting the papers. Sharon slapped her in the face — then felt searing remorse, cried, and hugged Annie very hard.

When Sharon was a child, her mother had often slapped her in the face when she was disobedient. She continued to do so until Sharon was a teenager and threatened to hit her mother back if she did not stop. Sharon always hated this sudden surge of temper in her mother and had vowed to her dolls during play that it would never happen to them — and, of course, never to her own children. Then, faced with work pressures and a deadline that was hard to meet, she had acted like her mother. The ingrained pattern worked automatically when the situation triggered it. Sharon had to work on restraining this automatic response tendency.

Sharon became aware of another problematic response. According to this pattern, she found herself resenting Annie after they'd had an especially good time together when she had showered Annie with kindness and generosity. Annie did appreciate and love her mother. Nonetheless, sometimes Annie's affection did not seem to be enough of a reward for Sharon. What she was actually resenting did not become consciously clear for some time. Then Sharon realized that she resented the fact that Annie might have a better mother than she had experienced. Astonishingly, Sharon realized that she felt a rivalry with Annie for having what her own remote mother had denied her. "How irrational can you get?" Sharon said to herself when she found she could verbalize this attitude.

This process of recognition led Sharon to understand the grievance she had been carrying unconsciously since her own childhood. "That was then, this is now!" she told herself. She was trying to be a good mother to Annie and felt that this brought something into the world that she had been denied. Adopting this attitude allowed Sharon to reprocess and retell the story of her own childhood. Her goal was clear for the future: to try to be as good a mother as possible to Annie and not repeat her childhood grievance.

Sharon's growth as a mature adult involved mourning. She had to give up a fantasy that she now realized could not become a reality. The fantasized ideal scenario was that, even now, as an adult, she would find ideal, restorative, and reparative mothering. Childhood was over for her, and she had to let go of redoing that sequence in her life. She could now experience and enjoy Annie as her daughter, without rivalry and envy, living in her true present and not her past.

## Impulsivity

If a child soils himself or wets his bed, he expects that his parent will perhaps scold him but will also set matters right by cleaning him up. If the parent appears and lets the child stay in the mess "to teach him a lesson," then the hope for help from the parent is dashed. As another example, a child may attack rather than play with another child in the playroom, while the parent ignores the bad behavior. Repeated interactions of this sort can be internalized as a self-state in which the adult views the child's behavior as uncontrolled and other people as unwilling to help.

As an adult, this trait of being an uncontrolled child leads to mounting frustrations and explosive hostility. A sense of continued grievance against power figures who have failed to be of support and help may persist into adulthood. The impulsive traits include being easily offended and outraged. In effect, the adult is still like an uncontrolled child who gets angry at the parent for just standing by without helping and lashes out. Such traits can be checked, reappraised, and altered in the direction of more self-monitoring, expanded self-governance, and increased coherence.

## Despondent Traits

When you find yourself satisfied with the repeated and unpleasant absence of someone in your life, you may also find that you judge yourself harshly. Another prevailing attitude from childhood might be an expectation of embarrassment and criticism.

There are many ways to positively criticize a child. An acceptable means is to carefully point out a specific behavior while avoiding disparagement of the child as a person. At an opposite extreme, a parent may ridicule and shame the child as a person.

A parent who struggles to avoid self-disgust and social shame may obscure his or her own role as a participant during troubled times, placing all the responsibility for the problem on the child. By always blaming the child, the parent can feel superior and may even derive sadistic pleasure from it. Repeated interactions of this sort lead the child to develop both a degraded self-concept and an adult tendency to make harsh self-judgments on themselves. A related behavior is that whenever a child fails to please others, she expresses intense scorn for herself.

## Perfectionistic Traits

To avoid shame and ward off a degraded self-concept, some children learn to reverse the parental criticism role–relationship model: They become the harsh judge who demeans someone else who is found to have fallen short of some perfectionist ideal. The adult character trait of habitual fault finding in themselves and others can be the result of an enduring habit of hypervigilance in placing blame for imperfections, rooted in an unconsciously undermined self-schema and a tendency to deliver harsh shaming statements.

These character traits of perfectionism and fault finding are often associated with self-doubting thoughts, the kind of unproductive review of situations and choices that actually prevents clear decisions. The situations that lead to these episodes are usually those in which there is some ambivalence about complying or not complying with the wishes or rules of others.

Spasms of self-doubt may cloud thinking in some self-states. You may feel overly confident and strong, and then suddenly flip to feeling weak and self-critical. The mind shuttles rapidly between contradictory intentions. Shall I submit? Shall I resist being controlled? Am I being really weak? Am I coming on too forcefully? With all these alternatives, no decision can be reached. Trains of thought become convoluted, cloudy, and confusing. Some books on personality call these obsessional traits.

A way out is to slow down and work to develop new ways of threading through dilemmas. Comparing choices is not easy. Some people are helped by writing down "what if" scenarios, such as, "What will happen if I act on this desire?" and "What will happen if I use restraint and don't act as I wish?" The positive and negative consequences of choosing each option can be added to the scenarios. After assessing the options, we can jot down possible compromises.

For example, you can jot down, "There is no perfect solution. The best choice is to delay acting until I have X in hand, Y has stepped aside, and Z shows interest. Waiting will feel tense, but I can tolerate that — it is my best option right now." Keep these notes on paper or in your mind. Then when the same old topic resurfaces, you can read the decision again and again. This reinforces rational choice making and reduces the intrusiveness of the topic.

---

## *Self-Status*

The world is full of hierarchies. To adapt well to society's rules, we need to learn to take direction and accept restraint without feeling weak, bad, or degraded by the act of submission. We benefit from knowing when and how to teach, lead, supervise, and take on responsibilities with conviction and continuity over time. It is also helpful to be able to enforce important principles without degrading others or becoming overly controlling of them.

People who want power but fear its consequences cannot enjoy success in attaining a relatively dominant position. When in power, they may become inconsistent in their treatment of others as a result of sudden feelings of weakness and the urge to escape feeling vulnerable. They also cannot feel satisfied when they are under the jurisdiction of others, so when they do submit to supervision or rules, they do so ungracefully.

Anger at being subjugated and fear of reprisals for resisting power are common emotional components of the next scenario.

## Bert: Courting Failure

Bert, a dental student, struggled with power and control issues. Although he did well in basic science courses, he had difficulty with authority figures — in this instance, the faculty in clinical dentistry. His trouble extended to all areas of his life. He did not remain in any relationship for long, even with friends. When dating, he engaged in power struggles that others found irritating.

The consequences of his attitude about power were especially grave in his dentistry program. Bert was now in danger of failing school. His supervisor evaluated him and found his paperwork substandard. All the students complained about completing the many records and forms, but Bert was seen as a rebellious leader raising tension between students and supervisors over the issue of recording timely reports into the electronic dental records.

Realizing he was close to losing sight of his career goals, and having been advised that his personality characteristics were also an issue, Bert sought psychotherapy. He told his therapist that he sometimes felt that doing the reports was irrelevant to either providing client service or gaining instruction for himself. He knew rationally that it was necessary for the survival of the clinic that payment for services be obtained through the insurance reports, but when he sat down at the computer to fill out the forms, he felt as if he was weakly submitting to the authority of his supervisor and wasting his own time.

As the therapy progressed, Bert grew more conscious of the problematic patterns in his behavior. When asked by the supervisor to bring the forms up-to-date, he sometimes complied submissively but other times turned stubbornly neglectful, belligerent, and sour. In the latter case, he immediately felt that he had gone too far and subserviently apologized. The instructor was irritated with both his resistance and his obsequious submission: Neither response was true cooperation.

Bert tried hard to make himself do the reports, setting up times and schedules for this task. Seated before a computer, with his fingers on the keys and his notes at hand, his thoughts shifted elsewhere in a confusing manner. He sometimes saw himself as capitulating meekly, slavishly filling out forms about diagnoses and procedures. At other moments, he felt he was being too harsh because his categorization of his patients according to the dental numerical codes seemed cold and inhumane. He then felt as if he did not care enough about their problems, but was only obtaining money for the clinic. Bert procrastinated, allowing a great many reports to pile up. But disregarding the forms left him in great danger. On one hand, avoiding routine paperwork made him feel like an idealist moving decisively ahead without submitting to bureaucratic nonsense. On the other hand, he could see his refusal to fill out the forms as a sign of low competence and status — he was unsure of his ability to make the correct formal diagnoses and assign the most appropriate treatment codes. In a catastrophic fantasy, he appeared before a faculty committee and was exposed as a child playing at being a dentist.

Bert reported that, as a child, he had felt too harshly controlled by one of his parents. He had stubbornly resisted the domineering demands, and his parent had then backed down, letting Bert gain control. From these interactions, Bert learned a tactic of continually thwarting authority figures, attempting to reverse who was in the power role and gaining the upper hand at being in control. However, this strategy failed him in adult life.

He began to revise his understanding of what could go on between people. He made an effort to seek out equal, cooperating, compromising, give-and-take strategies with peers and mentors. In particular, the idea of equal partners in an enterprise seemed new and revitalizing, both at work and in his marriage. Bert and his wife sat down together and discussed their problems. Both were helped by this good communication. Assertiveness and communication were key to this change.

## *Learning New Relationship Patterns*

We understand others intuitively unless we think carefully about what we are observing, what they are intending, and what motives may influence how they act with us. What they say is not always what they mean. Deceit or manipulation may occur. We decide who, when, and what to trust, as well when to maintain our safe boundaries or distance. We may want to change them, but really, we can change only ourselves and the relationship as "we" rather than "them."

To intuitively understand others, or ourselves with them, we unconsciously organize our perceptions, interpreting them and our reactions according to our role–relationship models. These are depositions from the past. They may fit the present or misrepresent what new opportunities actually exist in a relationship. When this happens, it is time to learn new ways. That often requires the work of consciousness, not just intuition, or stimulus/response thinking.

As we study the opportunities in a new relationship, we may feel a sense of tension, anxiety, or a little agitation because we are looking at unfamiliar possibilities such as more closeness and more caring, along with a greater risk of rejection. Learning requires tolerating this tension, while remaining appropriately rather than excessively cautious. The tension recedes with positive results, and with practice in making changes.

In a close relationship, we are often pressed by another person. That person is trying out his or her unconscious ideas and expectations of us. As a result, curious activation of our own unconscious processing can occur. What is happening is not just up to us; it occurs in clear and clouded exchanges. You can penetrate some of this inner and interactional fog as you are trying out something new for yourself. You can ask yourself whether what is being offered by you and the other person is 1) positive and 2) authentic. Is the other person reliable in the long run and positive and authentic in the present moment. Are you?

A harder question is this: Are you testing the other person, and is the other person testing you? Are there negatives or fears behind these provocations? Can you achieve trust and security? If you're a bit scared and want to back off, should you give in to that inhibiting urge? Can you take a little risk of caring and remain safe, as well as true to yourself?

Does this sound difficult? Take a look at the common situation. Many people fear rejection and become a bit socially phobic. They reject opportunities in order to avoid rejection, and they reject first to avoid feeling abandoned or uninteresting. This is just one example of how we share human dilemmas. Your conscious reflections are the best tool for making decisions when your intuitions seem too fantasy based, too impulsive, or too out of step with an actual chance to pursue happiness.

## *Points to Remember*

- Negative childhood experiences can lead to repetitive but unrecognized attitudes. Even positive childhood experiences can lead to ingrained attitudes that are maladaptive in adulthood.

- It is valuable to differentiate between a tendency to reenact prior relations and the possibility to reconstruct new ways of dealing with others.

- Practice new, effective ways to ask and negotiate for what you want.

- New types of interaction may feel uncomfortable at first because they are unfamiliar. Tolerating awkwardness of these new behaviors is important until repetition makes the new approaches to others feel more familiar.

# 6
# *Sexuality*

Sexuality is biologically driven and socially constrained. It's like viewing a play through a critic's eyes instead of allowing ourselves to interpret the story on our own. Erotic desires are not under our full conscious control, and our ability to feel sexual toward another does not always mesh with our individual conscious preferences or our social communities. Culture is complex, so our ideas about how to behave sexually are hybridized: Maybe our mother and father had differing views, and attitudes in our family and community may have clashed and been recombined over time. Among the multiplicity of sexual drives, wishes, desires, fears, and rules of right and wrong conduct, there's ample ground for elaborate psychological conflicts.

This complexity makes sexuality and interpersonal aggression the two most difficult areas concerning the reappraisal of attitudes. A mature person must make wise and considerate choices by using reason instead of rationalizations such as "It feels so good that I'll just go ahead and do it." Likewise, we can't merely hope that, by conscious choice, we can turn sexual desire on or off at will. Instead, we need to make responsible choices that govern how we express or restrain erotic emotions. For most of us, sexual appetites of the moment do not always reconcile themselves with our prevailing ethics, rules, vows, convictions, values, and morality.

Forming appropriate attitudes of self-governance also fosters integrity; both are important aspects of self-harmonization.

Even when we restrain our actions, we may have particularly recurrent sexual fantasies. We may have no intention of acting upon these desires, but we may find our fantasies to be unwanted intrusions into our consciousness. If so, the fantasy usually conflicts with our moral convictions. Some religions claim that these kinds of conflicting thoughts are sins. Others say, in essence, that the problem lies not in what you think; the sin arises only when you choose to act. Of course, the same applies in our systems of justice: It's not a crime to have ideas; it's a crime to do harm. The issue, once again, is self as agent in achieving emotional regulation.

## *Sexually Related Attitudes Are Learned in Childhood*

We don't all arrive at adulthood with the same attitudes about sexuality. When we look back into the past, we can learn lessons that help guide our choices in the future and aid us in revising our patterns for governing our sexual attitudes, emotions, and actions.

From a young age, we are taught limits about acceptable sexual behavior and gender roles. Conflict among anatomy, psychology, and social attitudes can make sexual development stressful. The result may be changeable or volatile character formation or a susceptibility to self-doubt — and even a presentation of self to others that feels inwardly inauthentic. As adults, we must sort out our values and carefully reconsider our personal needs through a filter of maturity and wisdom.

Some cultures dictate strictly feminine or masculine inclinations. In such a society, a girl who wants to become a sports hero may say to herself, "No, I must not — that sport is too masculine, and it will make me sexually unattractive." Likewise, a boy who wants to be a ballet dancer amid rigidly prescribed gender roles may frustrate his own desires by saying to himself, "No, that is too feminine and people will laugh at me." As a general rule, the more mature a person gets, the more he or she can accept having traits that society views as related to the opposite gender. Men can enjoy baking cookies without feeling that it's too feminine and can let go of the more restrictive notion that a man's place is at the barbeque grilling steaks.

## Sexually Problematic Attitudes

Sexually problematic attitudes are often held deep in the mind, as a secret shame. Even contemplating or daydreaming along these pathways of sexuality can be a source of anxiety or embarrassment. These emotions prompt avoidance of clear thinking, yet clear thinking can reduce shame. Understanding problematic attitudes reduces the shock of traumatic memories of sexual abuse. Thinking them over demystifies erotic fantasies. Thought is not the same as action — it's a way of trying out possible actions and can help us decide what to do.

People have a wide range of sexual wishes, some based on biology and some based on culture. Finding partners with reciprocal desires isn't usually easy. The goal is achieving personal safety in pleasure while avoiding any kind of harm to others. Within that scope of mutual consent, maintaining self-esteem requires maintaining values.

The most troublesome attitudes that persist into adulthood are rooted in childhood sexual abuse. These situations may involve seduction, sadism, or forceful assault. All these leave the child with self-schemas that involve elements of confusion about sexuality. They also promote dissociation of a caring parent from an exploitative or uncaring parent, even though these divergent roles belong to the same person.

Forceful assaults, in which the child feels frightened or hurt, can result in a role–relationship model in which the self is a weak, vulnerable, and/or violated child and the other is an overpowering figure. Many people overcome the conception of themselves as victims, but some people experience sexual inhibitions or dissociative states as adults. For example, during erotic situations, a person can have shifts in states of mind from excited eroticism to fear and shame.

Some degree of sexual abuse occurs in perhaps as many as one-fifth of childhoods. When the abuse is by a parent the child loves, the young mind faces a difficult problem. For example, a girl may develop a role–relationship model in which her father is a selfish molester who traumatizes her as a helpless victim. The daughter may also need to see her father as a kind protector who loves her, as a parent should.

The father in this kind of situation usually has both positive and negative approaches and care-taking functions. He is sometimes a good parent and sometimes a bad one. The state variation fosters contradictory self-states in the child. As a result, the child may preserve dissociated role–relationship models into adulthood. The child no longer can easily view herself as a cohesive individual.

Though I used the more common example of heterosexual paternal abuse of a daughter in this example, the same kind of role–relationship schematization can occur between a father and his son; likewise, the aggressor can be a mother abusing the same- or opposite-gender child. Uncles, aunts, older siblings, religious leaders, and other figures can be involved as well.

Some sexual violations are not traumatic for the children at the time they take place. They may enjoy the fond attention and even find the sex pleasurable. They may mistakenly view the abuser as a loved and loving figure. Only later do they see, with great rage, that the abuser was actually a selfish aggressor. Such instances become retrospective traumas. A state of horror may ensue when a person realizes, perhaps months or even years later, that a violation of trust occurred.

In hindsight, some of us may realize that the abusive parent was irresponsibly and reprehensibly unprotective. This can form a devastating sense of grievance and cause us to form revenge fantasies at an unconscious level. Unlocking these unconscious attitudes may help, to reappraise the whole story and realize that it happened in the past. Current relationships need not reenact aspects of that bad scene, with seduction followed by abandonment and betrayal.

These child abuse memories may be more than a diad between victim and aggressor. A third party also may be involved. For example, if a father uses a daughter sexually and the mother does not step in to protect the girl, the child may view the mother as failing in adequate caretaking.

Attitudes of grievance and even revenge then target both parents. Such grievances usually manifest more as an unconscious motive to get even or strike back at such figures than as a conscious plan for the life ahead.

Childhood sexual trauma has at least three possible lasting consequences: The child learns the role of victim and expects to repeat it; the child learns the reciprocal, aggressor role through identification and may enact it in later life; or the child finds it hard to reconcile the extremely different parental roles of caretaker and abuser. This may impair the child's self-organization and ability to love and trust another person in a friendly sexual relationship, because, at least unconsciously, the child fears victimization. In addition, sometimes an intruding critical "figure," called an *introject,* seems to speak in the victim's mind. Such introjects may invade the sexual sphere of conscious sensations in the form of visual images of that person's face or auditory images of his or her voice.

Sexuality is inextricably connected to moral mandates. As an extreme form of bodily intimacy, sexuality can be threatening. Sex can hurt, transmit disease, and create an unwanted baby. Sex can involve domination, with one partner excessively and aggressively controlling the other. Empathy, compassion, and even rudimentary kindness can be lost during sex. Sexuality can be blunted or infused with hostility that the victim rationalizes by blaming the other person for being remote or not providing enough satisfaction. This aura of blame and accusation can shatter intimacy.

Children who are emotionally, physically, and/or sexually abused often believe (either because they've been taught it or because they assume it) that their innate "badness" has caused their terrible circumstances. A child also might sometimes be faulted simply for asking to have his or her own needs met and, from then on, has difficulty expressing his or her wishes. The child may even feel unentitled to live out a heartfelt dream.

## Sadism

Matters are even worse if sadistic roles were enacted upon the child. Through a reversal from weak and passive roles to strong and active roles, the child can learn to be a sadistic aggressor. Later, with traits of sadism, the person derives pleasure from assuming an aggressive role and subjugating, degrading, or even injuring another person. Part of the gratification may come from exerting power over the degraded other. In some milder sadistic sexual practices, the vulnerability is only feigned, to arouse excitement. The humiliation and pain is part of the play instead of real mortification of the partner. As we know, there's an enormous legal and moral gap between having a willing and an unwilling sexual partner.

Aside from whatever biological drives may exist, sadistic sexual role–relationship models can be reinforced by a prior failure to learn schemas that contain scripts for mutual caring and gratification. A sadistic script might dictate the irrational expectation that when one person signals erotic interest, the other rejects the partner as uninteresting or even repulsive. Anticipating rejection, the person can then respond with rage. A sadistic attack on an unwilling other reduces the shame and self-deflation of feeling rejected. Sadism can take the form of rape, serving, in part, as revenge on the other for a perceived lack of desire.

For some people, sadistic role–relationship models are part of a search for excitement, using the thrill of aggression within and the fear instilled in the other to overcome the lack of erotic excitement they associate with normal sexual practices. Sadism provides a route to the kind of excitement they need for orgasm. They must learn to restrain such selfishness.

## Voyeuristic and Exhibitionistic Role–Relationship Models

Voyeurism and fantasy can also involve elements of hostility. Looking, a normal component of sexual arousal, becomes the major vehicle for voyeurs. Viewing another person against his or her will is a form of victimization. Exposing the self to show off and solicit interest is another normal component of sexuality that can be excessively exaggerated because of limitations in arousal. A person might exhibit him- or herself in a variety of ways, enjoying the belief that the victim is violated by being forced to look.

## Masochism

The masochistic role involves expecting some kind of satisfaction by submitting to the will of a powerful partner, as when lovers allow or even ask their partner to tie them up or use handcuffs. At times, the vulnerability is part of a script that begins with as-if declarations, such as, "I am not responsible or guilty for submitting to the pleasures that are about to be given me." In the script, fear or pain may even be a kind of necessary prepayment to excuse wanton exhibitions of the bodily self to gain the attention of the other. When carried beyond cooperative mutual play, such fantasies can destroy tenderness and true caring. However, new, nonsubmissive erotic attitudes can be learned by repeated conscious reflection, social support, and new experiences.

## *Erotogenic Fantasies*

Sexual thoughts often include fantasy. During either masturbation or intercourse, private mental fantasies serve as a way of increasing excitement, even when they do not accurately depict the actual partner. Sex play can include acting out roles of mutual fantasies when the actions are negotiated and shared. Acting on dangerous fantasies, however, is a value transgression because it might harm someone. We have to take responsibility and exercise self-restraint, even warning ourselves ahead of time to avoid acting on impulses of the moment. Imagination reduces repetitive risky forms of excitement seeking. That is, in safety, one can imagine one thing while doing another. Avoid others who would lure you into dangerous adventures or drug-altered states of mind.

### Larry: Risky Forms of Erotic Arousal

Larry experienced sexual pleasure and orgasm only if he was crawling through a window into a house in which he had previously seen a woman whom he didn't know. The risk of possibly being discovered in an illegal entry added to his excitement, but eluding discovery was also part of the storyline. Thus, Larry always chose a time to enter when no one was home. As he imagined the woman at home, the window took on another meaning and symbolized her sexually opening to him and willfully admitting him to intimacy. In entering the house through the window, he was symbolically entering her — but he was also forcing her to submit to his desire. Larry was committing criminal acts in this isolated sector of his life. His freedom and security were in great danger.

Why did Larry achieve orgasm only when he acted out this dangerous story? Why did he not simply masturbate in his own room using a fantasy that followed the same script? For him, fantasy during masturbation was not sufficiently "real," yet seeking out a woman for a normal sexual relationship was too frightening. He assumed, probably correctly, that a real woman would reject him. He needed just the right amount of reality for his excitement and sense of thrill (crawling through a real window into the house of a real woman), balanced with just the right absence of reality (no woman actually present and no male rivals for her attention) to evoke a fantasy-based sexual excitement.

Larry learned that he liked to play a strong role with wicked overtones, to strengthen his disturbed sense of frail identity. He needed to learn how to become a man with enough confidence in his relationship and sexual capacities to derive satisfaction from real, shared experiences and companionship with vibrant and self-asserting women. This would take time, attention, help, and hard work. Meanwhile, he had to stop rationalizing his criminal acts as okay because he didn't "hurt anyone, steal anything, or get caught." He had to learn to exercise restraint over his "game" of entering real windows of real homes.

Sexual conflicts like Larry's may seem foreign to you, but hopefully I've reduced the shock value of naming topics that do pertain to some readers. Sorting out sexuality and moral conundrums is a universal aspect of self-understanding, even if the actual conflicts vary widely.

## *Overcoming Passivity*

Sometimes we let ourselves be used sexually as an easy way out of dilemmas in which we fear rejection if we do not respond to the urgent wishes of another person. If rejected, we fear the self-states of becoming lonely and lovesick. Such submission seldom works well as a plan. For example, Sarah tended to do whatever her boyfriends said they really wanted, and really needed, because they loved her so much. She hardly knew she was acting on a fear of their anger and rejection. She did not exercise enough self-care or find a way to negotiate for what she wanted and really needed.

We need to summon the strength to talk to those who are aggressive or abusive toward us and to endure the state of being alone if a relationship separation occurs after an unsuccessful negotiation and successful protection of self-boundaries. If we get stuck in a pattern of repeated cooperation with a domineering other, it's time to examine why these cycles seem adaptive when they are really maladaptive.

## *Marriage and Values*

Marriage is a social institution that evolved in most cultures to harmonize our inevitable conflicts about sexuality, reproduction, child rearing, and domestic arrangements.

Understanding personal views about marriage is part of integrating all the aspects of the self. One goal is to develop capacities for the kind of integrity that can fulfill pledges.

Personal views range from the romantic idealizations of adolescence, including images of perfect lovers destined by fate for each other, to the condemnation of any pacts of closeness, on the grounds that one's parents had a terrible marriage. Expectations of being trapped in an irresponsible and uncaring marriage can destroy the pursuit of happiness. Re-examining your parents' marriage may help you better understand where your views came from and ease the transition to more realistic views.

A realistic view of marriage emphasizes a commitment to shared values. This is where sexuality intersects with issues of affiliation and a continually caring attitude. Part of figuring out one's views on fidelity involves finding a balance between a self-centered pursuit of pleasure and a couple-centered mutuality of attachment that may require restrained erotic urges toward nonpartners. This is a particular area where self-understanding can increase by verbalizing and writing out personal attitudes about right and wrong, good and bad, clean and dirty, selfish and committed.

Because sexuality can be amplified by fantasies and sublimated in a variety of ways, it is an area where values and moral conflicts come into play. These values, which we learn quite early, become intuitions. We have hunches about what we should or should not do, and many of us even have rules about what we should or should not think. My repeated message is that self-understanding in conflictual topics means trying to put these strong hunches about what is right or wrong into words. The best compromises on what to do and what not to do are reached in this way. Verbalization leads to the clearest rules for continuing self-governance and a future plan for when and how to say no.

Becoming aware of previously unconscious attitudes and then consciously forming new ones can counteract irrational beliefs with more moderate, nuanced views. By putting desire into words, we can find associations with other words that clarify restrictions and commitments. We may find that we can see our rationalizations for previous wrong actions in a clearer light. Character growth comes with facing moral dilemmas and making rational choices that strengthen good connections with others and increase self-respect.

## Clarifying Personal Boundaries

For a relationship to work, each person must respect the boundaries of the other. In adult relationships, boundaries protect intimacy. Every person needs respect; individual needs, feelings, attitudes, and values must be recognized and acknowledged. In a good partnership or marriage, much is shared, but not everything. Some couples preserve intimacy by agreeing to disagree on certain irreconcilable differences and respecting each other's privacy in that regard. Some couples maintain separate bank accounts, observe different religious practices, pursue different hobbies or social lives, and support different political parties. Friendly respect for individual roles and beliefs bridges differences and maintains closeness. It stands to reason, then, that violating boundaries is one of the surest ways to destroy intimacy.

When a parent crosses the line with a child by being sexual, violent, or neglectful, the law recognizes such treatment as abuse and prosecutes the offenders. In adult interactions, violations may not be so clear. And some of us, for the sake of avoiding conflict, are too passive about establishing and defending the perimeters of our safe space. It helps to recognize the inner signals of a boundary violation: a flare of tension, fear, or a sense of backing off in response to a specific behavior by the other person. These may be only flickers of minor distress, but they are worth considering as part of a repetitive pattern of discomfort. It is wise to clarify these signals, at least in the privacy of one's own mind.

If you are in a troubled relationship and you want more intimacy, take a careful look at how you and your partner have drawn your boundaries. Clarifying and tweaking your shared and separated spaces may help you create a closer connection.

Issues about boundaries and attitudes toward sexuality and intimacy often arise when circumstances change. As we enter new chapters in our lives, we can be presented with opportunities to confront and examine our old beliefs, to rewrite our mental map for relationships yet again. New parents, for example, typically find that they aren't completely in sync about how to care for and raise their infant. These differences may be based on how they were raised and which of their own parents' attitudes they want to avoid or emulate. How they handle these disagreements can enhance or ruin a relationship, as many couples have discovered.

Earlier negative experiences in relationships, whether they occurred when we were infants, children, or adolescents, make us all vulnerable to engaging in unsatisfying and destructive patterns with everyone in our lives — especially with our own children, relatives, and close friends. By recognizing this vulnerability and engaging in a little self-monitoring, you can plan and appropriately adjust your own behavior to counteract your old impulses. You can be a better parent than your mother or father may have been. You can be a better spouse or a better friend. Your values and judgments can evolve. You can replace an intuitive behavior with a new, conscious moral principle; grow in maturity; and find your way to greater harmony.

## *Points to Remember*

- Recognizing a pattern that does not work in the long run is the first step in reworking maladaptive eroticism.

- Sexuality can lead to short-term, intense pleasure and long-range, destructive consequences. Protect yourself for the future possibilities. Learn to govern and restrain yourself where needed for self-care. With time, such self-governance becomes more conscious, more competent, and less rigid.

- Self-understanding includes attention to realms of fantasy and imagination. Expressing these realms in words enhances rational, conscious thinking.

- Feeling entitled to pleasure can be a selfish form of rationalization and, in the long run, can result in discontent and loneliness.

- People vary in their attitudes about sexuality and their capacity for intimacy. Some of this variation is due to endowment, some to life experiences. In general, early traumas may make it harder to develop deep and constant affiliations later in life, but reviewing and revising your attitudes and later good experiences can improve and dispel fears that traumas will be repeated.

# Part III
# Processing

# 7
# Consciousness and How to Amplify It into Insight

Many times, we can learn to amplify skills for reflective awareness, to better grasp our attitudes. In essence, we're shining the spotlight on skills that build an understanding of both conscious and unconscious meanings and processes of changing beliefs. Conscious intentions can modify our unconscious expectations. This is not instant — it takes repeated effort, just as an actor must practice his craft. In the theater of the mind, this effort means learning how conscious thought can, in effect, look at itself. To delve deeper into this, we can consider modes of awareness.

The top level of awareness is *reflective consciousness*. From this higher platform, we review what is going on in lower-level, *primary consciousness*. Most of us mentally dwell in the realm of primary consciousness during most of our waking hours. In reflective consciousness, we repeat a sequence of thought found in primary consciousness and then compare and contrast alternative attitudes about it. This method of reflecting is often called *introspection* or *mindfulness*. New conceptualizations reached through use of reflective consciousness are called *insight*.

In primary consciousness, we have a sense of words and images that translate sensations into feelings or moods. The flow of experiences seems like little movies in the mind's eye. We also have a third kind of consciousness — and, keeping with my metaphor, a lower kind of awareness — that is a *peripheral awareness* of what is happening. In peripheral awareness, our ideas are largely perceptual and spatial. We can elevate them to primary consciousness by adding symbols such as words. Through repetition, we can move these into reflective consciousness. Then perhaps we can answer questions such as how and why we have particular ideas and how and why emotions color our peripheral awareness.

In reflective awareness, and in a calm and attentive state of mind, we are best able to differentiate realistic from fantastic appraisals of what things mean. Differentiating between reality and fantasy is a major way of reducing confusion and modifying appraisals of previously habitual and perhaps immature attitudes. The process of reflective consciousness, judging ideas that we first thought about in a stream of primary consciousness, is called *metacognition*. The clarity of ideas produced through this process is called insight.

## Larry and Insight into Jealousy

Larry had a repeated train of primary conscious thought in which he felt that his parents had given his sister more money for her graduate college education than him. For example, when visiting her apartment, he noticed she had a nice new desk and chair set. He had a stream of ideas and mental images as he drove home, contrasting her cool-looking, modern corner with the rickety, secondhand, seriously scarred table he'd crammed into his own apartment. In his peripheral awareness, he noticed a sensation of clenching his jaw. In his reflective consciousness, he wondered why he was grinding his teeth as he processed these thoughts. Larry duplicated his stream of primary consciousness. Reinterpreting the flow of ideas and images led him to label his self-state to one of himself as loser envying the transactions between his parents and his sister. He put this self-state into words: *I envy my sister. I resent my parents giving her more money as support. Am I justified?*

In his reflective awareness, Larry took a position of explicitly challenging his judgments. His implicit attitude was connected to many memories, facts, and fantasies, each with their own actualities and distortion of facts. Instead of reflexively feeling envy and resentment, he reappraised his attitude about the family issue. He did not have to enter a harshly critical self-state of "people who envy are terrible people." Instead, he could appraise from an equidistant attitude of experiencing feelings and evaluating what had evoked his ideas. Larry remembered how his parents had given to him as well as his sister. They had nurtured and given to both in different ways, for many reasons.

In this way, Larry was able to use his reflective consciousness to separate reality from fantasy exaggerations.

---

## *New Decisions*

Conscious reflective awareness allows us to make a careful and rational choice between opposing alternatives. We can compare incompatible plans, consider which one is preferable, and then decide how to act. In such contemplations, we can sometimes merge contradictory views and contradictory goals to arrive at an adaptive compromise, and this can increase self-coherence.

Anticipating various possible consequences of an imagined scenario allows us to choose the best option. If we reacted lamely to a challenging situation, we can review the memory, consider other alternatives, and then decide on a more appropriate mode of reaction. We can then practice it with conscious care until we've repeated it enough to form a new habit of response to that kind of challenge.

For example, if someone frequently goads you into a hostile argument, you can think through the pattern ahead of time and decide that such banter is unpleasant and a waste of time. You can consider how to handle such provocation in the future. You might plan to be alert to your companion's provocations and use self-monitoring to urge yourself to react neutrally, negotiate, and/or present an alternative topic for conversation. In time, the new pattern of response will become habitual because it works in a rewarding or protective way. You will come to reinforce and embrace it as a new attitude.

Reflective awareness can include both a loosened rein on imagination and a conscious intention to use verbal reasoning to examine whatever we imagine. We can contemplate a challenging situation in different scenarios: an ideal outcome, a poor outcome, and then a more realistic set of consequences. For each of these possible outcomes, we can use imagination to freely explore the potential actions and potential consequences. We can question and reexamine cause-and-effect suppositions. In this way, imagination enables us to expansively think about and explore "what it all means."

## Judy: Contemplating Envy

Reflective awareness can help us unpack the attitudes that lead to a medley of feelings. Envy, for example, is a complex collection of emotions that can combine aspects of anger, longing, and sorrow.

Judy, a graduate student, suffered from low self-esteem and an intense envy of more successful women. She hated them but also felt sorry that she was not more like them. Judy learned how to tackle the pervasive problem of envy by using conscious reflection to unpack memories of numerous but small episodes of states she had experienced and named as jealous self-states.

Although Judy felt shy around men her own age, she met an appealing man in her seminar and hoped they might get to know one another better. He looked at her with interest, but he also seemed shy about making the first move. Karen, a popular woman in the class, sat next to him one day, introduced herself, and got into an animated conversation. Judy envied Karen for her poise and courage in talking to this classmate.

As she later reflected on Karen's attributes, Judy saw Karen in her mind's eye as "poised, good-looking, and courageous." Judy could even enact the image in her mind of Karen's demeanor, imitating the posture and facial expression of Karen's patterns of engagement.

She compared her attractiveness with Karen's and found her own appearance less appealing in her imagination. But when put into words, her attitude of "I am really ugly, no one could want me" was clearly irrational. She then more reasonably labeled Karen as somewhat "prettier" than herself. Judy had an imaginary image of herself in Karen's place, beside the man, and felt a flush of anger that Karen had usurped her in this position. She experienced this anger as a bodily sensation, first through tension in her fists and then consciously as a rush of heat to her face.

Judy realized that, in her mind, she expected that she would never be able to summon up the courage and poise she had observed in Karen. That attitude made her sad, but she could change her expectations. Her sadness contained the concept that things would never go well for her. She counteracted this unrealistic idea with the concept that she could learn to be poised if she tried hard enough and practiced conversation skills.

She could then challenge her more dreaded self-views with new, realistic self-appraisals. She could see a tired look on her face in a photograph or in the mirror without jumping to the erroneous, pessimistic conclusion that "things will never go well for me" or that this would decrease her value as a worthwhile, intelligent woman. Thinking and self-talk helped Karen reconsider her attributes around the important topic to her of being attractive. She told herself that she was basically an intelligent, creative, nurturing, attractive person. She could give up on her all-or-nothing thinking habits and build up her self-confidence by consciously replacing negative, stereotypical ideas and images of what it meant to be a woman in the society in which she had grown up. She could practice new skills and augment her social roles. Over time, and using reflective consciousness, Judy was able to reduce feelings of envy (as Larry did in the earlier example). She replaced self-pity with assertive and well-reasoned plans for possible future relationship successes.

## Paul: Learning to Reflect and Verbally Express Feelings

Early in developing conceptual skills, learning to reflect in words what we are doing is hard in and of itself. We sometimes need help in acquiring this skill of verbalization. In some cases, we follow a sequence from acting out feelings in social behavior, then learning to speak rather than act in social communications, and then learning to use more words in the mind itself. In a sense, we learn how to learn more through reflective consciousness.

Fifteen-year-old Paul had recently begun to steal, drink heavily, and conspicuously cut class at his high school. Eventually, he was placed in an adolescent rehabilitation home, but he began to break the rules there, too. He brought in a bottle of wine, lied to the staff, and challenged the rules.

These actions made it clear that Paul was acting out the role of a rebel, particularly in his attempts to provoke staff members into reacting angrily toward him. When they finally did react, he told other staff members about the "retaliations." Paul's pattern of behavior in the rehabilitation facility recapitulated his role in his family, where he'd tried to create a wedge between his father and mother. Underlying Paul's manifest toughness was his own inadequate sense of identity.

The staff recognized and discussed Paul's pattern of provocation. They developed a consistent approach to dealing with his behavior. They patiently called Paul's actions to his attention by labeling them as the kind of actions they experienced as menacing. This allowed Paul to realize that his actions had consequences. When the staff asked him about his goals, Paul said that he just wanted people to "back off" and not bother him. The staff pressed him to come up with actions that might better serve his needs. They helped him learn to phrase his needs politely, as in, "I would just like to read in my room right now. Would you please leave so I can do that?"

This type of dialogue helped Paul learn how to establish verbal communication. In the tense environment of his family life, he had never experienced negotiations in which both parties worked together to talk about their motives. For a time, Paul felt increasingly uneasy. Gradually, he developed better, more trusting relationships with the staff, and their positive reactions helped him develop more positive feelings about himself. He began to speak about his sense of being weak, his anger toward his parents, and his fear of becoming an adult. The staff responded with optimism. They pointed out that he was learning new, useful attributes and expressed confidence that he would be able to handle home and school life in new and better ways in the future.

Paul gained conceptual skills as he learned to verbalize his intentions and consciously formulate his wishes. As he learned to communicate his emotions, including his urgent, angry sense of frustration, he started to feel more in control. His increased capacity helped to bolster his sense of confidence that he could leave the facility and find new ways of connecting with peers, teachers, and employers. Paul had gained skills in reflective self-awareness.

## *Intrusive Thoughts and Unexpected Pangs of Emotion*

For many of us, calm self-states can be interrupted by unintended deflections. Intrusive episodes increase in frequency and intensity after stressful events that we don't know how to handle. Unwanted images also emerge more frequently with fatigue and inner conflict. For example, Clara was feeling fine until distressing images derailed her conscious daydream.

Clara had begun to find her marriage dull and uneventful. She was looking forward to attending an upcoming party with her husband because she hoped it would brighten her attitude. She and her husband both livened up in social occasions with other couples, so she hoped a night out together would do their relationship good.

One night while her children were asleep and her husband was still at work, Clara was making a party dress for herself. She was sewing stitches that required only a minimal amount of attention. She fell into a daydream that began with a pleasant image of wearing the completed dress to a cocktail party, visualizing how its vivid yellow material brought out the warm tones in her bronze skin. She imagined the glowing admiration of the socially prominent hostess. She then imagined a man coming over to talk to her because she looked so lovely. In the daydream, Clara and the man continued conversing on a walk in the garden. Then she imagined that she was a widow and that this walk led to a kiss, beginning a new romance. At this point, Clara ended her daydream abruptly and she felt upset that she had imagined her husband's death as part of her fantasy.

When we drift into a daydream, we tend to feel liberated from our usual commitments or restraints. We imagine, "What if I was free to do the following?" But Clara's daydream led her to fear that she might wish to be free of her husband. The prospect of handily eliminating the major obstacle to a romantic encounter was too close to Clara's recent but restrained impulse to find a new source of romantic excitement. Clara was aware that she was the one shaping the daydream and felt guilty. Her thought process led to shame and shock, as if she were wishing for her husband's death. It helped Clara to realize that fantasies are not plans — and surely not magical causes of actions.

While fantasies and dreams can be useful in what they indicate about our unconscious motives, we are not as morally responsible for them as we are for our actions. We are free in our imaginations and responsible for our dreams only if we choose to act on them.

What bothered Clara the most was that her primary conscious stream felt in control at first and then veered beyond her control. She consciously noted with alarm the point at which it felt out of control.

Clara had an intrusive primary conscious experience. While intrusions may make us uncomfortable, they often indicate an issue that needs more attention. Clara used reflective awareness to repeat and analyze her thoughts. She paused to consider her conflicted feelings about her relationship with her husband and thought about how she could reactivate excitement within her marriage instead of passively taking dullness for granted.

Intrusive thoughts sometimes come more as unbidden images than sequences of verbal concepts. Traumatic flashbacks are another example in which intrusive thoughts arise. For example, a worker who experienced an explosion in a factory may yet perceive the sounds, sights, and smells of the incident, even weeks afterward. There would be immediate coping with the event and its consequences. Such intrusive episodes are signals to pay attention to the psychological fact that aspects of the traumatic event are still being unconsciously processed. Sometimes such traumatic repetitions also come back to consciousness during sleep, in the form of dream images.

## *Dreams*

Dreams are the primary consciousness working as a stream of images during a state of sleep. Some dreams we remember upon waking, but most we forget. At the psychological level, most dreams are inscrutable and occasionally startling. A few dreams stand out as having symbolic meanings. A man once dreamed of a giraffe lying on the ground, its long neck looking like a limp snake. In the dream, he had an idea that the neck looked vulnerable, as though someone might step on it. He awoke, a bit anxious. He'd had the dream the night before he was to participate in a panel discussion at a public meeting. The dream images were a complex visual warning against possible embarrassment: "Don't stick your neck out."

Dreams may depict aspects of the self. For instance, sometimes we dream of ourselves as a child or as a decade younger than now. Dreams also may contain topics of concern in our secondary consciousness during the previous day. A dream about a car rolling more rapidly downhill, for example, might symbolize a fear of losing control in impetuously pursuing a goal. The person who had this dream might go on to dream about trying to close a door on a dirty room or walking an unruly dog that tugs at its leash. All these scenarios depict actions that respond to a threat, serve as a warning, and act as an incentive to protect the self. The message is, "Stay in control." Anxious people frequently dream of houses catching fire, of falling, or of being menaced by monsters, all scenes in which they are too paralyzed or too slow to escape.

Although it is not unusual to have an occasional nightmare, some people have recurrent bad dreams. Nightmares, extreme forms of anxiety dreams, are common in post-traumatic stress disorders. Their message is often essentially, "Don't sleep! Danger is again all around you! Be alert!" or "Don't rest, you still have terribly important business of unsettled memories — don't forget them!"

Sometimes while asleep, we are able to have reflective consciousness — that is, to know that we are dreaming and to make some types of judgments about the dream images flowing by. This kind of experience is called *lucid dreaming.* In some cultures, the skill of lucid dreaming is advocated. For example, an elder suggests a topic before sleep, perhaps in a family discussion while conversing together at dinner. The suggestion promotes creative thinking, perhaps on how a particular problem might be imagined as having some solution in the future.

We usually forget our dreams, but efforts to remember them increase our ability to retain some of the dream details. If and when that occurs, we can use reflective consciousness while fully awake to try to understand some elements that we recall. This is more likely to be useful if we repeatedly experience the same dream or dream patterns over weeks or months. Sometimes dreams of traumatic memories can recur many times.

We can clarify the meaning of specific repetitive dreams by exploring our associations while awake to each element that we remember in the sequences of the dream. In reflective consciousness, we newly appraise the dream and its associations. If the dream was a bad dream, we can try to forge a new, less nightmarish conclusion through contemplation. Sometimes this changes the course of the future repetitive dreams.

As in the discussion of lucid dreaming that we just considered, one has lucid wakefulness about a dream. One starts with the dream memory and then bends the sequence of images in the wakeful mind's eye toward less catastrophic events and some way of coping with the monsters, invasions, or persecutions in the dream. With children, this has been called making a pet or friend out of a dream monster. For adults, it gets complicated but can be worth the repetitive efforts if you are experiencing a recurrent bad dream or theme.

As with problematic behavior patterns, we can use reflective consciousness to formulate alternate, more adaptive solutions. Then we can use insights we gain from interpreting the dream images to work through the fears we're expressing in the dreams. In the case of repetitive bad dreams, we can, before sleeping, reassert in reflective consciousness a revised and positive scenario. We can intend to have less frightening dreams — but this is not an easy or inevitable solution to bad dreams.

## *Revising Conscious Opinions*

Many enduring attitudes and attachments are embedded patterns in the unconscious mind. Some are dynamic, in that their activation leads to emotional motives, and these motives can influence mood. We revise or counteract unconscious attitudes and opinions by using reflective consciousness. Revising conscious appraisals can change unconscious attitudes.

We have touched upon this possibility for reappraisal in every chapter. Here we review some ways of dealing with troublesome topics that come to our conscious attention with a bit of intrusiveness, indicating that the topic is unresolved. I call these intrusions or jumbles "hard topics."

Hard topics include stressful memories and moral dilemmas. They come into primary consciousness repeatedly. You can use reflective consciousness to work through these hard topics, to make them less intrusive.

The steps in the following outline can help you reconstruct your ideas. Writing in a journal can help as well as you use your own version of these ten steps.

1.  Select a hard topic, with these characteristics:

    • One that has a tendency to often intrude into or worry your mind.

    • One with pangs of intense and confusing emotions, a medley of feelings you intuitively know you should slowly and eventually unpack.

    • One that keeps you from making effective plans for moving on with certain aspects of your life.

2.  Get into the right frame of mind.

3. Create a calm state in which you give yourself time to proceed slowly. Relaxation exercises may help, such as clenching and releasing muscles or taking slow, deep breaths.

4. Establish an intention to think clearly and openly, while avoiding harsh self-criticism.

5. Aim at thinking, as well as thinking about how you are thinking.

6. Stop and do something else if your calm disappears.

7. Set goals for the revision of your attitudes. What do you hope to achieve from your period of contemplation? These suggestions may be helpful:

- Use dose-by-dose thinking. Don't expect that you will come up with an absolute solution in just one session.

- Plan to be "not too sure" about your conclusions in a given session. Keep an open mind.

- Plan to remember and return to your key ideas.

- Clarify the various aspects of a hard topic.

- Give each subtopic a name so that you can find it later in your mind.

- Write down the ideas, feelings, and values associated with each topic.

- Establish cause and effect. Expand the hard topic's meanings. Include your intentions and expectations.

- Describe the intentions and expectations of others.

- Include your reactions to others' intentions and expectations.

8. Examine contexts and scenarios of what is likely and unlikely to happen:

- Best (idealized) versions

- Worst (dreaded or catastrophized) versions

- More realistic or middle-ground versions

9. Separate reality from fantasy.

- Challenge your current appraisals with alternative ones.

- Reconsider the attitudes you have toward your own roles and toward what the stressor events mean for your future. Consider what is preventing you from moving forward.

- Be rationally optimistic. Don't give up or give in to an easy but inappropriate choice as a quick way out.

- Prioritize your own values.

- State your principles.

- Put them in order, from most to least important.

- Choose a path of gratitude, compassion, completion, and forgiveness.

10. Make realistic decisions.

- Focus on plans for the middle-term future.

- Imagine following these plans in various contexts.

- Practice new actions. Expect them to feel awkward at first. With repetition, they will come more easily.

## *Points to Remember*

- Learn how to use reflective conscious awareness as your best tool for solving dilemmas, making your best choices, and planning ahead to reach your goals.

- Excessive flooding of consciousness with rage is especially disorganizing. Learn how to check yourself when a flare of temper disrupts reflective consciousness. Seek calm before planning how best to react to insults and injuries.

- Relying on prior attitudes can introduce errors of judgment about the real intentions of other people. New appraisals and interpretations may be needed.

- Thinking about your new decisions repeatedly can help correct intuitive but dysfunctional attitudes.

- Clear, calm, and warm verbalization of what we want, feel, and fear can increase success of negotiations in intimate relationships and prevent unnecessary ruptures in an otherwise sound connection

.

# 8
# *Unconscious Processes*

The unconscious workings of the mind seem very large, like a huge and complex set of cameras with the switch permanently set to the on position. They hum along in the background, capturing an enormous array of information that we experience through our senses and by automatically observing everything in our environment every day, whether we're awake and asleep. Only some of the information processed gains conscious representation. Of high importance, unconscious information processing assesses who we are and whether we feel threatened. When signals indicate a threatening situation, the constellation of thoughts and feelings crosses a threshold. Consequently, we pay more attention to aspects of that constellation, as now represented in consciousness

Emotions such as alarm and anxiety motivate us to pay even more attention, to evaluate and solve potential problems. But sometimes the emotions of alarm, fear, anxiety, shame, guilt, or rage can become too intense. We evaluate this intensity of feelings and *potential* feelings unconsciously. Such intense emotions as rage and fear threaten to disorganize our realistic thinking and action planning.

Intense feelings can sometimes disorganize our thinking. Some inhibitions of memories, fantasies, perceptions, and ideas occur unconsciously to prevent such disorganized states by reducing emotional excitation. Some traumatic memories and threats may then get buried in unconscious information storages. This situation is not ideal; we are better served when we consciously process and master our experiences. Over time, however, we may still be able to work through past experiences that we previously buried. As we become stronger through adulthood, we become better able to process buried childhood information.

Much of our discussion in this chapter centers on altering attitudes held in our unconscious organizations of meaning. We want to watch for situations in which attention gets blunted when it might better be sharpened; in such cases, avoidances are excessive. We also want to focus on the other extreme: directing too much attention to threats based on conditioned and prior fears that are now unjustified by real circumstances. Interestingly, these are the extremes seen in post-traumatic conditions: too much denial and too many intrusive disruptions of conscious concentration.

Unconscious processes examine many threads of information. New stimuli are matched with various forms of enduring memories and schemas. Mismatches between mental expectations and what is perceived as happening tend to generate emotions. Fear is the prime example if the mismatch leads to negative premonitions; joy is the prime example if outcomes are hugely better than what was anticipated with dread.

The unconscious processes work rapidly and in parallel. The conclusions of information processing may work out differently: One channel may devise an answer about what the input means; another channel may not. Imagine that several stages are in motion and the same basic scenario is being produced on each of them. The drama has different outcomes. Self-reflective awareness can compare and contrast the outcomes. Unconscious processes will already have done this, so only a few of the results get consciously examined. Puzzling interpretations can be thought through, using consciousness as the special tool to logically appraise them. Meanwhile, conscious intentions can influence unconscious processing of information. The current self-state influences both conscious and unconscious processing of incoming information, or emergent memories that have not yet been fully processed. The activated self-schemas are organizing principles, and the processing can change which self-schema is activated, and how overall self-organization can be transformed.

## Unconscious Self-Organization

As we discussed in Chapters 1–3, on identity, most of the information about our self-organization is stored and processed unconsciously. We may have different self-schemas and role–relationship models. These organize the kind of parallel unconscious information processing just mentioned.

Unconscious information processing can determine whether some threat to self exists. If threat is computed as a possibility, we may react emotionally. If the stimuli are alarming enough, we experience it consciously, through physical sensations, intuitive forebodings, intrusive images, bad dreams, or words. We may also feel a variety of identity disturbances, such as depersonalization or a sense of identity diffusion. These alarms and disturbances may motivate us to pay conscious attention to how we can solve salient problems.

## Unconsciously Stored Memories and Fantasies

Some alarms seem strange. We may have an unnamable anxiety related to unconscious schemas or to sets of associations, called memories. For example, traumatic memories sometimes resurface after an apparent absence from consciousness. We may experience them through formless unease before they become clear in our consciousness.

Even if we consciously intend to remember something, we may lock away a memory that was previously in consciousness so that we may not be able to immediately recall it to our conscious mind. For example, after the death of a loved one, a husband may want to recall his wife's face at a happier time but finds that the images will not come. This tends to occur early, when grief seems overwhelming in its potential emotions and degraded self-states. In the future, after mourning has made the memory safer to contemplate, the images will more readily come to the surface in conscious thought. The information is not lost; it is inhibited in unconscious storages.

Memories and emotions are especially complex, entwined with interactions between conscious and unconscious mental processes. We can seldom know without some kind of other evidence whether a memory is true to an actual past experience. Memory is constructed and thus can be misconstructed. As you examine your life story, you will find you cannot be "too sure" about what really happened. You are writing, for yourself, a current narrative. To understand this, it is helpful to consider types of memories in a straightforward way. For our discussion, I've categorized the levels of memory as locked, active, and inaccessible. Unlocked memory can be retrieved with conscious intention to bring it into conscious clarity.

A *locked memory* could be brought back into consciousness if that memory not blocked. This kind of memory state was once called a repressed memory, usually the result of a traumatic experience. Our cognitive regulation processes have marked such memories as "forget all about this." For example, a memory of a drunken parent's abuse might be enduringly recorded, but conscious recall is inhibited. Although we lock up this memory because of its frightening and overwhelming impact, the memory is not gone; evidence that this event occurred may reside in our family history.

Under some circumstances, a locked-away memory may return to awareness. It is hard, however, to separate true memories from fantasized memories. Some childhood trauma recollections combine real and imagined elements. In fact, this inaccuracy of recall has long been involved in various legal and scientific controversies over what used to be called repressed memories.

An *inaccessible memory* is a previously processed form of information that has not been represented in words or images. Associations between threatening perceptions and high emotional alarm, pain, or distress may have been established only in preconscious processing. That is why we can encounter a reminder of a past trauma and feel a spasm in our stomach. It is because bodily associations are part of the stored information — the body knows how to prepare for a flight-or-fight response!

Associations connected in this way, with an inaccessible memory, can occur without our knowing why the conscious sensations draw attention. A particular odor, such as the smell of an intoxicated parent's breath, might trigger a headache. Only when some kind of causal, declarative thinking has occurred do we realize that this reaction signals a previously inaccessible memory of abuse.

Some aspects of memory are "active," in that they are marked for later conscious processing, even if these memories are also inhibited. In this way, they behave similarly to locked memories. A traumatic childhood experience may reside in this category of *active memory* and later return intrusively into our consciousness for further processing of meaning. This intrusive pattern continues until the memory has been sufficiently reviewed and articulated with our self-organizing narratives.

## *Freud's Early Concept of Repression*

The locked category of unconscious thought refers to memories, fantasies, or plans that have been blocked by some type of inhibition. In such a case, our mind does not wanting to know what happened or what might happen. Freud referred to such memories, fears, and desires as repressed. The inhibitory processes on an otherwise consciously accessible memory were defensive because they served a wish to avoid entering an intensely emotional, undermodulated, and dreaded state of mind.

Since Freud's time, we have learned that both conscious and unconscious mental processes are more complex than he hypothesized. Still, many of his insights endure, including his observation that not all memories that emerge from the locked category really happened as remembered; some are, at least in part, "false" memories.

## *Retrieving Warded-Off Memories and Fantasies*

Locked away, but still active on a deeper level, memories can be unlocked by first establishing a safe atmosphere. Associations that relate to the memory may also dispel the inhibitions that are blocking this memory. The result may be unbidden images or intrusive thoughts about a long-past trauma or fantasies about a traumatic experience.

As just mentioned, inhibitions are there to prevent the danger of entry into dreaded states of mind. Containing danger within a secure place in the unconscious mind can reduce threat and lead to focused attention. Distressing emotional states can still occur, but they are usually within tolerable limits.

For example, perhaps you felt that the sorrow of a perceived loss from the past was too dangerous to experience. At some later point, you may yet feel safe enough to emotionally thaw out from frozen grief. Then when sorrow seems tolerable, the memory that you warded off can reach your reflective conscious awareness. An incomplete mourning process can move forward toward a point of more completion. Along the way, you might experience distress from fear, rage, guilt, and shame, but these self-states can be self-owned and within tolerable limits. That is, you can move beyond intrusive images and denial-numbing into a process of working through difficult topics that you previously warded off.

## *Conscious Influences on Unconscious Processing*

Most of the time, we can consciously move our attention from one topic to another. Sometimes, however, we do not have the skill to do it and may feel out of control. Other times, we find that our conscious attention is diverted from our chosen focus. When intrusive experiences occur, we can later come to understand why this was the case, as I did in this example.

When I was a medical student at the University of California–San Francisco, I was making ward rounds with my teacher, the chief medical resident. We entered the room of one of his patients whom I was to examine and diagnose. As we stood by the bedside, I felt my pulse suddenly quicken. I entered a state of anxious hypervigilance and wondered why I had the jitters. I was simultaneously aware of the odor of a rarely used antiseptic but attached no immediate significance to the smell. I also had a sense of déjà vu, the uncanny feeling of having been in the same kind of situation before, although I had never been in that hospital room or seen that patient.

I concealed my fear and examined the patient as I had been taught. My jittery state of mind did not subside until we left the room to continue our rounds. Later, I contemplated and analyzed my reaction, trying to connect all the elements of the memory. Only then, and over about a half-hour of calm contemplation, could I reconstruct a much earlier memory associated with the peculiar smell of that antiseptic.

As a child, I'd had throat surgery for an infected abscess. I'd shared a room with an airplane pilot whose face had been badly burned in war. He had undergone major plastic surgery to reconstruct his mouth, and the surgical wound had become infected. I had also had a complication, a post-operative hemorrhage, and was terrified that I would become as badly disfigured or near to death as this man was. The smell of the antiseptic in that childhood hospital room was the same as the odor that had recently triggered my reaction, and it had been associated with the traumatic fear I had experienced as a child. This had happened long ago, and I had not thought of the unfortunate pilot and his terrible wounds until the specific odor of the antiseptic activated the memory. An unconscious thought process had associated the odor with that memory and triggered my fear.

My first conscious reminiscence of myself as an adult medical student in that hospital room was of my own bodily reaction of alarm. The emotional reaction based on unconscious associations was virtually instantaneous. However, I did not consciously recognize the particular meaning of the odor until much later.

The association of an emotional reaction (in my case, the alarm emotion of fear) with a stimulus that accompanies a particular state of mind has been called *conditioning* — in particular, classical conditioning (by Pavlov, in 1928, and Skinner, in 1953). The smell of the antiseptic was not a threat to me; the image of myself as facially disfigured or dying was what had terrified me. But the smell had occurred at the same time as my distraught state of mind and was now part of a schema, or mental model, that aroused fear when operative. The emotion I felt, through bodily and image representations, first brought the childhood model to my consciousness.

Such as shift in state of mind from calm to jittery, through unconscious thought, is not uncommon. Bringing the associations into consciousness is part of the routine of psychotherapy. The conscious reflection does not erase the unconscious associations that lead to emotion and mood changes, but the understanding — and, hence, the expansion of meanings — enhances a sense of self-mastery. How did I shift from a calm state to an alarmed state, and how could I gain control of my reaction? A series of stages of occurs to assemble meaning, awareness, and new understandings when confronted with a sudden shift in state of mind. Let's consider them, using my own experience as an example.

As I entered the hospital room, I was in a "competent medical student" state of mind. I was in a mentor–mentee relationship with a competent doctor, and we were working together with cooperative patients who needed and received medical care. I was calm and alert. I was not aware of any sensations of rapid pulse, increased heartbeat, knotted stomach, or muscle tension. My perception of the antiseptic odor was mysteriously inconsistent with these attitudes because it was also associated in an important way with elements of another schema.

The other schema involved memories of a traumatic event in my past. That schema also involved hospital rooms, patients, doctors, and this particular odor. But in that context, I was a frightened child facing harm or death in relation to others who were perhaps not competent enough to protect me. This alternate working model triggered, at a neural level, my fearful state of the jitters.

The association of the odor to the "vulnerable child" schema set off an unconscious reaction of alarm, a sudden alerting response in preparation for the possible repetition of a dangerous situation. The reaction of alarm led to bodily changes and then to my conscious sensations of rapid pulse, tightened stomach, and muscle tension. This whole pattern marked a transition from my state of calm to one of the jitters. The resulting hypervigilance led me quickly to check all my surroundings for danger. This confirmed the working model in which I was a competent medical student, not the patient, and the doctor in charge was my competent mentor. I suppressed any actions associated with my tension and jitteriness, such as rapidly gazing about the room, and inhibited the trains of thought associated with my anxious response until a later, more appropriate time. Instead, I focused on my tasks with the patient.

When I suppressed my anxious reaction, I stored the memory in what is known as active memory. Active memory functions as a storehouse for what needs to be reconsidered. The word *active* is used because the mind, even without conscious awareness, stores puzzling but highly relevant information in memory stores beyond the usual transience of short-term memory. Functionally, the mental processes of assessment flag the information as needing more attention later because of its importance to the self.

When we take time for calm contemplation without outside interruption, we create the opportunity to bring the contents of our active memory into consciousness, where we can review and reinterpret it. The memory and fantasy-based information stored in active memory can then be meshed with our most mature, up-to-date, and harmonized self-schemas.

Conscious emotions can be unpleasant. Certainly, I did not want to feel jittery when I was about to examine a patient in the presence of my mentor. To reduce undesired emotions, we can work to control our thoughts. I was able to partially mask my anxiety by monitoring my thoughts and feelings. I became aware that I might look scared or distracted, which would not be a professional stance. Using reflective awareness, I was able to compose my face and calm my voice and demeanor.

Such control measures can operate unconsciously. The unconscious mind is looking ahead, modeling potential consequences, and making regulatory adjustments as a result of what it anticipates. In my case, I was unconsciously thinking ahead about how my mentor and the patient would react if I displayed fear. I was then able to opt for a more situationally appropriate response.

A person with hyperactive fear circuitry might not have been able to suppress the surge of alarm that I felt in that hospital room. Instead, panic might have resulted, accompanied by an irresistible urge to flee the scene. In those circumstances, the action would be followed by intense shame. That result might then reinforce a fear of hospital rooms, leading perhaps to a phobia of such environments. The phobia, in turn, would trap the individual in a vicious cycle because succumbing to the phobic impulse would be incompatible with being a medical student. The eventual outcome could be leaving school, becoming depressed over failure, having an impaired self-concept with deflated self-esteem, and withdrawing from challenges that would normally bolster self-competence.

Earlier, I mentioned unconscious processing of information in parallel systems. Various schemas may be used in this processing. It will probably be most adaptive if a person activates a component and realistic self-schema to organize thinking about incoming and potentially stressful information. Yet earlier self-schemas may also be activated because they seem similar to current emotional situations. When our ability to keep higher-order self-organization in a primary position is reduced, such as when we experience high levels of stress, fatigue, intoxication, or illness, we may not use our most advanced self-organization to process information.

The important point is that conscious thought can sometimes override some unconscious associations of a stimulus to an emotional response, as when I decided not to reveal my inner panic when I smelled the strange odor but was also under observation for my performance as a medical student. To an extent, conscious choice can modify unconscious attitudes. Unconscious attitudes may function as if to say that we cannot process a traumatic memory and it should therefore remain buried or off-stage. Our conscious attitudes can say, in effect, that we can safely recall and reassess the memory. We can examine how to interpret it now, in relation to what it means for us in the near future.

Your intentions to examine warded-off content usually require becoming aware that an unconscious control is operating. This seems paradoxical: How can consciousness know what unconscious mental processes conceal? Some signals supplement intuition that something is being concealed in the theater of conscious thinking, as flutters from off-stage characters wanting to come onstage and express themselves. The topics that intrude into our attention from off-stage may get shoved back again because their emotional contents threaten our well-being or calm. However, safe, deliberated efforts to bring a scene to the forefront of consciousness helps us better contemplate the material.

Training the mind to understand patterns of conscious and unconscious controls can help us develop valuable new mental skills and modify habits of inhibition or distortion of certain types of ideas.

## *Restructuring Your Life Narrative in Times of Change*

After a serious life event, we often need to reassess various beliefs, feelings, and attitudes. By this, I mean subjecting even distressing memories to reappraisal, reinterpretation, causal analysis, and rational examination of different possible choices in the future. In undertaking such a review, we often find that unconscious processing contains potential trains of thought that are not based in reality. Two extremes may arise: one a catastrophic, fearful, worst-case scenario set of associations, and the other an overly idealistic illusion of total mastery, such as when a fairy godmother grants us all we need. Rational contemplation falls between these extremes.

## Amy: Finding the Midpoint between Catastrophic and Overidealized Trains of Thought

Amy anticipated a promotion, with a hefty increase in salary and new leadership duties over the sector of a corporation in which she worked. She was well respected by superiors and supervisees. Yet the economic collapse of markets affected the organization. The leadership post and the entire sector were phased out, and the relevant business was sold to another corporation.

Amy was shocked. For a couple days, she felt numb. Then she got all the facts about her layoff and what might follow, including unemployment insurance. She set to work applying for a new position. During this period, she had intrusive thoughts of a repetitive nature.

One set of thoughts was catastrophic: Her finances would be totally exhausted. The state would stop insurance, her house would be repossessed, and she would be thrown onto the street, never to recover. People would despise her. She came to realize that the images in this scenario came from documentaries of the Great Depression. Her parents had suffered during that time and had told her similar stories.

A second set of thoughts was extremely unrealistic but gratifying — idealizations of what might happen. The company that bought the business sector she had occupied would fire the person who ran the relevant division because Amy was so great they just had to have her. While she imagined the extremely unlikely offer and acceptance interview, she consciously examined both sets of thoughts as extremes: catastrophic and idealized. This labeling enabled her to sit down at her kitchen table and lay out both facts and probabilities in a systematic way. That exercise led to forming realistic plans and expectations.

## Steve: Using Deliberate Choice to Counteract Habitual Avoidances

Steve was a surgical resident at a crucial level of training that would dictate his future career. During this training, the faculty surgeon with whom he worked told Steve that, in spite of his diligent efforts at practicing techniques, he was not meeting the required standards of skill in performing surgeries. In addition, even more practice might not produce the fine motor skills required. This feedback was very bad news for Steve. For years, he had entertained the ideal fantasy of eventually becoming a great surgeon.

The discrepancy between the new information that he had only mediocre skills in key areas and Steve's prevailing knowledge that he needed great surgical skills to succeed in his chosen profession threatened to bring on a painful emotional realization. He unconsciously anticipated the danger of entering a dreaded state of mind: the intense feelings of shame that would accompany the admission of his failure. To avoid this shameful state of mind, he inhibited his thoughts, which kept him from realizing the implications of the faculty surgeon's remarks. Steve selectively ignored suggestions and feedback from his mentor, unconsciously chose not to contemplate the conversations later, when he was alone, and also belittled the opinions of the chief when speaking to other trainees.

Steve's maladaptive avoidance strategies were defensive compromises. His mood was stabilized at a tolerably positive level, but at the expense of not contemplating useful information about the reality of his professional skills. The reality was that, even if he continued to practice to develop surgical skills, he might not progress well in this specialty. By thinking carefully, he could plan to exit his current track gracefully and pursue another specialization that would utilize his ability to listen well, interact with patients, and make excellent diagnostic assessments.

Using conscious and unconscious control processes, we can modulate the emotional consequences of processing information that we might otherwise find difficult to accept. The results may be adaptive when we process emotionally evocative information in smaller, more tolerable doses. If Steve had contemplated the full range of potentially catastrophic consequences of the negative feedback from his supervisor, it would have been an emotional avalanche. If he had considered his father's condemnation of his failure, his shame in front of his friends, his potentially disastrous future, and a variety of experiences of incompetence from grade school, his stance of defensive coping through avoidance would have crumbled. He would have been devastated by an uncontrollable storm of intense emotion.

A tolerable dose of information, by contrast, is adaptive. Steve considered just one topic: his choice for moving smoothly into a new specialization track in the short-term future. Instead of having either catastrophic or dose-by-dose adaptive thinking, Steve was actually procrastinating rather than dealing with his situation adaptively. His avoidance strategies, developed as a means of self-protection, ironically prevented him from maintaining his self-esteem and garnering the respect he would have gained from others in the long run if he pursued a more fitting career track.

# *Understanding Excessively Repetitive Patterns*

Because of our unique life experiences, we all have a certain repertoire of knowledge about ourselves and others. The kind of role–relationship models discussed in earlier chapters reside within and can be activated from this usually unconscious repertoire. You may feel powerful because of an unconscious view of yourself as inordinately strong. At other times, you may feel fragile and vulnerable because you unconsciously view yourself as inordinately weak. Neither of the extreme views may be an accurate rendition of yourself as you are now, with an actual body of bone, muscle, and capacities. Your goal is to activate the most competent, realistic self-schemas.

Information in one unconscious subsystem of associated meanings may not connect with another unconscious subsystem of meanings. In this case, strong and weak self-schemas do not average out and ameliorate each other as they might in a more harmonious self-organization. Conscious reflection can rectify such separations, enable us to develop more inner repeated harmony, and check ourselves at the very beginning of what might be a maladaptive pattern of relationships.

As we use conscious reflections to re-examine previously automatic attitudes and responsivities, we find ourselves asking a good question: What else could we do in this kind of situation? We may consciously plan a better pattern of reaction to stimuli that might provoke us to do something we would later regret. But this plan is a *new* course of action or inner feeling; it is not as familiar as the old, maladaptive pattern.

The conscious choice to try something in a new way may require many trials and efforts that at first feel awkward and even risky. Part of change is forming an intention about how to implement new decisions. If we carry out this intention and examine the consequences of the new plan over time, we may gradually (but not instantly) produce beneficial results.

Consider awareness as a first step and insight as a second step. Forming and implementing the new plan is the crucial third step. Then in addition to the benefits of not repeating an outworn attitude, you acquire an expanded toolkit for reasoned thinking and self-control.

This point bears repeating: Awareness in consciousness can lead to the use of thinking as a tool for solving conflicts and reaching a narrative that connects identity over time: past, present, and expectations for the future. Table 8.1 summarizes this path from awareness to insight and new choices.

**Table 8.1:** *Awareness, Insight, and Decision Making*

|  | *Awareness* | *Insight* | *Decision Making* |
|---|---|---|---|
| *Self-States* | Knowing when a change in mood occurs | Understanding how and why a change in mood occurs | Planning how to avoid entry into problematic states |
| *Altered Unconscious Controls* | Recognizing avoidance | Realizing how and why the avoidance occurs | Choosing to focus attention on and rework the buried topic |
| *Attitudes* | Knowing attributions of self and others | Finding differences between old concepts of self and new concepts of self based on new experiences | Choosing and rehearsing new roles for the self |

## *Points to Remember*

- Intentions govern the flow of thought processes.

- By forming a conscious aim to think calmly using reflective awareness, a person may increase a sense of safety in examining difficult topics. This may allow locked memories to be more fully processed.

- A more coherent sense of identity and relationship continuity can be developed by relating past to present and future time frames. A previously split or dissociated fragment of memory can be gradually integrated with a larger narrative about self.

# 9
# *Controlling Undesirable Emotional States*

Whether as actors or audiences, we all experience certain self-states that we want to personally avoid: guilt, fearfulness, despair, and rage, to name a few. To escape, we may use conscious or unconscious methods of shifting attention away from an emotional train of thought that threatens to overwhelm our control. Avoidances help us stabilize our self-cohesion. However, avoidances may prevent us from resolving our conflicts within that hard topic. We can use reflective awareness periodically to decide when to continue distracting our attention from an alarming topic and when to contemplate a dose of it.

We may prevent memories, fantasies, ideas, and emotions from reaching conscious representation for a variety of reasons. Recalling a traumatic memory can evoke intense feelings. Reviewing a rejection or abandonment can lead to so much anger that rational thought processes become disorganized. On the other hand, using reflective consciousness, we can work memories into a reasonable interpretation that fits into the narrative of our life so far and our possible future plans.

A memory of a past event changes over time. Each review can lead to a somewhat different version. We mix what happened with what we think happened. Some is real, some may be an appraisal, and some may be a mind image that seems like a perceptual or "actual" image.

In each version of a memory review as deposited back into our various memory storages, we add the appraisals and judgments that occurred during the review process. Early versions may have the best appraisals of the time, but a memory from childhood or adolescence does not have the appraisals of our adult minds. This is good news. We can transform our narratives about the past, working on them in the present. New expectations for the future also occur. Were we once abused, we need not always expect abuse, and so shun the risks involved in close relationships with others.

## *Improving Deliberate Attention Control*

Learning to pay attention in a productive way includes practicing skills for engaging and then, if too much emotional arousal occurs, disengaging and moving to another topic. To use reflective consciousness effectively, we have to develop the ability to come back to the first topic at a later point. The most common avoidances simply stop the progression of ideas. Instead of clarifying our theories or perceptions, we say to ourselves, "I don't know" — or, in other words, "I don't want to know."

When you observe your thoughts stopping, you may want to pay attention to the idea you just had and consider what might have been the next idea. Ask why the inhibition occurred. Other good questions include two variants of a threat: Why would that be distressing? and what would be a feared consequence of the ideas and emotions if they became real?

## Ellen: Selective Focus and Topics of Attention

Ellen, an architect, was planning the construction of a building. She consciously made the effort to think about her project step by step. She chose to think about the immediate design step instead of her need for the fee, which she would collect only after the blueprints were approved. She did not want to get distracted by thoughts of the flood two years ago that had destroyed her car, garage, and garden, and created a financial strain on her family. For Ellen to cope effectively during her office hours, she needed to concentrate on the design problem. After she earned her fee, she could later think about what the disaster might mean for her present and her future.

If Ellen had thought intrusively about the flood, she might have been unable to concentrate on the current step for designing the building plans. However, if she never thought about the flood, she would be denying that something important and threatening had happened to her. Controlling her focus of attention meant finding an appropriate time to think about each of the various topics weighing upon her present plans — and her future.

---

## *Psychological Defenses*

We make unconscious decisions about the anticipated emotional effects of expressing our thoughts consciously and expressing both our feelings and our ideas socially.

These unconscious decisions can lead to consciously sensing an anxious mood. Often the underlying threat remains obscure. Many people find it valuable to find out why, how, and when they are stifling a possible train of thought.

Each of us may use particular psychological defenses as part of our personality traits. We can even learn that we are doing so. This is best done through reflective self-observation, to review a previous state of mind. And it is best done by finding what we habitually tend to do as an avoidance or distortion. A quick review of the general terms used in the past may help you more consciously control your attention, especially how to counteract habits of avoidance and distortion. By intending to think reasonably and calmly about difficult problems or traumatic memories one can revise unwanted attitudes.

## Suppression

Some emotional control processes, such as suppression, are quite conscious. Suppression shifts attention away from a distressing topic though deliberate, conscious choice. For example, we may turn our minds from yesterday's fender-bender to instead think about the good meal we will enjoy at next Friday's family dinner. We're essentially saying, "I will forget about this for now." We put the unresolved topic out of mind because we cannot solve the problem at that particular time and the associated emotions are too distressing. Suppression is the least maladaptive defense because it is conscious. It only becomes maladaptive if one always avoids thinking over a hard topic, and so never comes to any new, rational decision about it.

## Rationalization

In rationalization, we defend our sense of good identity by giving logical reasons for actions that we actually performed for other reasons. The most common motivation underlying rationalization is the desire to avoid self-blame. Rationalization is also used to justify avoiding unpleasant duties, such as not ever washing the dishes because one is having potentially great creative thoughts while sitting on the couch and watching TV.

## Repression

A traumatic event can lead to repression, or unconsciously withholding from conscious awareness a particular memory, fantasy, idea or feeling. *Repression* differs from suppression, in that it is involuntary; the inhibitions occur unconsciously instead of as a voluntary process.

Repression can take the form of an inability to remember an important but traumatic event, as is the case with amnesia. Alternatively, repression can curb disturbing wishes, ideas, and feelings that have not yet reached consciousness but would emerge if not for the avoidant process. For example, a person may repress an awareness of potential erotic arousal toward a person for whom an expression of sexual love would be inappropriate, or may repress hatred for a person one "ought" to love, such as a grandparent who has been harshly punitive and critical.

## Denial

Denial is one of the most frequent ways to control upsetting ideas and prevent a dreaded emotional state. For example, upon hearing that war is descending, a person might try to achieve peace of mind by assuming, "It can't happen here." Denial involves withholding our conscious understanding of the meaning and implications of what we intuitively perceive as significant new information.

The magical thinking in denial leads to an ostrich effect of sticking one's head in the sand, as if avoiding the problem will make it disappear. Although some denial is healthy because it facilitates a gradual acceptance of bad news, denial becomes problematic if it interferes with dealing rationally with threats to one's physical well-being. In such cases, denial can be harmful, as when a physician experiences the kind of pain associated with a heart attack but goes right on jogging, to prove that he is healthy and that the symptoms are illusory.

## Idealization

Idealization results from a need to have a relationship that inflates our own sense of worth. We imagine that we share values with someone we see as greater than ourself. For example, we believe that our political party has the right, that our army is blessed by the gods, and that our school is the best. This is defensive behavior: We believe that we have the attribute we are idealizing instead of learning to become principled and competent ourselves. Thus, attributing exaggerated positive qualities to a person or group we are affiliated with, whether real or unreal, gives us reflected glory.

## Displacement

Displacement occurs when we transfer ideas and feelings that we have avoided to some other person, situation, or object. As an example, after being reprimanded at work, a person may tactfully submit, yet go home and kick the family dog or yell at a child for a minor infraction.

## Dissociation

In the case of dissociation, we deal with emotional conflicts, or internal or external stress, by temporarily altering the way consciousness works to weave the disparate parts of our identity together. What is consciously known in one state of mind is segregated from what is consciously known in another state of mind. For example, a person who is deeply potentially embarrassed by a selfish act of stealing from a friend can forget for a time about the minor theft and remember the relationship only in terms of kindly sharing belongings. Memories of discord are as if forgotten, and only good memories of caring about each other are brought into consciousness.

## Intellectualization

To avoid the problematic emotional implications of a topic, some people intellectualize the subject and deal with it on a purely ideational level. A related defense, *generalization,* involves dealing with the topic on an abstract rather than personal level, to avoid excessive emotion. For example, in a conversation about having cheated while in an honored position of responsibility, a person may leap to philosophical thoughts about human imperfections in general, to distance himself from the personal feelings of self-criticism and remorse. Another common form of intellectualization dwells on tiny, peripheral, factual details instead of getting at the emotional heart of a topic under negotiation. For instance, a person might report having hit her child but then gets sidetracked by giving details of the clothing the child was wearing and why she selected the garments.

## Projection

In the case of projection, a buried impulse or idea is viewed as outside of self and, instead, located as if it were someone else's intention or aim. For example, people who struggle with their own self-hatred may develop a delusion that others are out to get them. This gives them an acceptable rationale for hating and allows them to avoid recognizing their own destructive impulses. Projection usually involves displacing onto the other person an aspect of the self that we do not want to acknowledge. For example, people who are avoiding their own hostility toward themselves may look for some vexing attribute in another person.

In a variation called projective identification, someone may provoke another person into becoming irritable. If the other reacts, one's own anger seems justified as a response to the hostile behavior. Now the self seems justified in being indignant and can view the other person as wrong. Provoking the other person into hostility provides a basis for blaming him or her for any argument or frustration.

## Reaction Formation

In reaction formation, a buried idea or feeling is replaced by an unconsciously derived but consciously felt emphasis on its opposite. For example, an older boy who is jealous of a baby brother might harbor a fantasy that if the baby died, he would again be the center of his parents' attention. Having had such a fantasy, he realizes that it is "bad" — in a sense, he has been "ordered" by his parents to love his baby brother.

Reaction formation consists of replacing the wish to be rid of his little brother with an exaggerated concern for the baby's welfare. If the substituted wish works, he cares for his brother even though he still occasionally wishes to be the only child again. If his conflict is too intense, the reaction formation may lead to problematic symptoms. For instance, the boy might feel a compulsion to check on the baby every 15 minutes throughout the night, to make sure he is safe from suffocating or being kidnapped.

## Role Reversal

In role reversal, the roles of self and other are switched. The usual reversal is for an individual to place himself in the strong rather than weak role. When in danger of feeling controlled because she wants to please a domestic partner, for example, a wife may become domineering and demanding, as a defense against seeming too dependent. Another common reversal is to remove oneself from the role of accused and instead become the accuser or critic, putting the other person involved in the blamed role. When domestic partners both use this defense, they may have volatile, mutually accusatory arguments that extend beyond reasonable limits.

## Barth's Troubled Marriage: Working to Modify Role Reversal as a Self-Defense

Barth hated to feel put down by his wife. When she tried to bring up the tense topic of renegotiating which of them was to take responsibility for various household chores, such as taking out the garbage, Barth routinely changed the topic to focus on some shortcoming of hers. In one instance, Barth dug up memories from their remote past, like the time they missed a flight as a result of her tardiness. Focusing on his wife's problems made Barth feel as if he had gained the moral high ground and was winning the argument. But this gain was only in his own mind, since his wife was frustrated and becoming increasingly remote from him. Barth's strategy was a problematic effort at coping using role reversal to blame his wife for everything. Obviously, this was not a successful means of negotiating.

Barth avoided experiencing his usual feelings of being accused, criticized, and ashamed by acting critically toward his wife. He exaggerated her shortcomings and minimized his own. His habits of self-defense created either uproar of mutual accusations or his wife's withdrawal.

On the brink of a serious rupture in his marriage, Barth realized that he had to change his behavior. He began to carefully pay attention to what was really going on in both his mind and his wife's mind. Barth found that he could improve his ability to listen to her and to their conversations. He then reviewed their past conversations in his mind and reduced his defensive posture. He increased the time he spent with his wife discussing her concerns and tried to really appraise not only what she said, but also what she needed. Barth found that he could work at responding in a new and more appropriate way.

## Splitting

In instances of splitting, one deals with emotional conflicts or internal or external stress by viewing oneself or others as all good or all bad. The process of dissociation segregates meanings, as if they belong in entirely compartmentalized, unassociated clusters. As a result, the positive and negative qualities of self and others fail to integrate into cohesive images. Someone who uses splitting may experience explosive state shifts, such as when alternately idealizing and devaluing another person. Likewise, a person initially in a cheerful mood may suddenly change to take on a mood of complaining.

## Undoing

Undoing expresses both an impulse and its opposite, as in being domineering one minute and deferential the next minute. Experienced in rapid repetition, undoing can lead to indecisiveness. For example, instead of complaining about the actions of another person and trying to negotiate an agreement, a person might start complaining and then retract, saying, "It is all my fault," only to switch back and forth between both positions again.

---

## *Defensive Habits, Attitude Formation, Defensive Modification, and Attitude Change*

Self-protection that works can become habitual. That is, if someone defends against threats, the ways of defense can get schematized, automatized, and built into the very fabric of our developing character. Projection, for example, leads to views of relationship roles that distort reality, but that can still be protective. Modifying attitudes gets complex, and we may have to address a whole set of traits to move our adult development to a good level of functional capacity. To illustrate this process, consider the following example of Les. This case study involves projections that became relatively fixed attitudes; they were both dysfunctional and defensive against even worse threats to his well-being.

Les came into treatment because but he routinely ended his relationships when he encountered even a minor frustration with the other person. He also felt chronic depression that seemed to stem more from self-esteem problems than from some kind of chemical imbalance. He was a workaholic without creative zest. Much of the time, he felt empty or lonely. When he met someone he felt attracted to because of his or her intelligence, interests, or appearance, Les tended to exhibit a paradoxical response if the other person also showed interest. Instead of feeling excited about the new contact, he felt irritable that what he or she was offering did not ideally suit his goals.

Les also felt this irritation when the other person seemed to want something from him, if only his company. He felt the other person was intruding into his time and even his mind. This new friend might deplete him. He then backed off and felt angry with the friend for not providing a better relationship. Les realized that his vexation was somehow unrealistic, yet it repeated the alienation he had felt from both of his parents during childhood and adolescence.

He repeated this pattern with me. If I was flexible and changed his appointment to a more convenient time for him, his response was paradoxical. Instead of expressing thanks, he appeared sullen and implied that the new time was still inconvenient in relation to his need to produce work and make money. Underneath this was what he called "a crazy attitude." He felt jealous of me, that I could be what he took to be generous when he could not be at all giving to others without feeling empty and depleted by their needs. He knew intellectually that this was an exaggeration, but it was a familiar one that seemed lifelong to him.

I responded by telling Les that he would have to challenge his attitude by unpacking all his ideas related to it. He tried to cooperate but introduced every kind of resistance, defiance, and deflection when we tried to discuss it. I patiently noted these and asked "why." Gradually, he explained that this "crazy attitude" was like a security blanket. It protected him from fear that he would experience some kind of warmth in a relationship, only to have it abruptly and painfully withdrawn.

Les wanted an ideal of eternal warmth and adopted a distant attitude to protect against the reality that no warmth is eternal. The first steps were for both of us to learn to tolerate this anxiety about counteracting the "crazy attitude" and becoming comfortable with the give-and-take process of listening to each other and discussing feelings. Knowing that an attitude is irrational is not enough; a familiar irrational attitude must be counteracted by some kind of new learning. This often means tolerating the tension that arises in engaging in new experiences of thought, feeling, and interaction with others.

It turned out that Les was still using attitudes he had developed as a child. If he got what he wanted, he was left alone, or abandoned. If he did not get what he wanted, he attacked whoever he saw as withholding the desired outcome from him. On the other hand, if someone gave Les the care he wanted, he felt too invaded by that person, as if he could no longer be self-sufficient and was being overly controlled. Most of the time, Les acted as if he felt normal. But although he acted responsibly and amiably, his inner world felt only dark and depressing. He feigned affection and said the right things, yet he did not feel authentically warm and caring. However, he could not maintain this act when the relationship got closer, when the other person revealed his or her mind to him and expected reciprocal disclosure of his inner feelings. Part of his darkness was the collapse of promising relationships.

Together, Les and I examined the moment of collapse in his relationships through repeated, careful review of his memories. He tended to have extreme attitudes that he called "crazy" because he recognized the irrational nature of that extremity. One extreme attitude was that the other person was too intrusive. When he or she tried to be empathic and get closer, Les felt emotionally and almost physically as if the other person was invading his mind and even his body (especially if it was a sexual relationship). On the other hand, if the other person moved in a way that Les interpreted as distancing him- or herself from intimacy, he interpreted remoteness as abandonment. He felt shaky and angry in response to either extreme; he felt a confusing medley of fear and hostility. Without much room in between invasion and relationship rupture, Les had to erect defenses to preserve himself as alone and intact.

Les had already learned how to curb expressions of hostility, although he felt it in his mind and shunned the other person as a kind of aggression. Now he had to learn to stay in the relationship without expecting to feel mutual warmth, while at the same time, accepting his fear. He learned to expect to tolerate the fear. Les then could see that he was not being abandoned: The other person was only having a time-out and would return to tune in to him again. Tolerating some threats of fear or embarrassment allowed him to learn new, small scraps of more authentic communion with another person. This did not erase his old ways, but it gradually reduced that fear into a not-so-dreaded and not-so-avoided state of mind so that he could seek truer contact with others. Occasionally, others responded by offering a more continuous and better relationship. Les's risky behavior of opening up had rewarding outcomes, which encouraged him to continue on the right path.

## *Points to Remember*

- We all control our moods by avoiding tough problems and stressful memories. If we do this to excess, however, we do not find solutions or acceptances. The best way to control attention is to consciously choose when to consider and when not to consider these themes.

- In some self-states, we unconsciously distort meanings according to our views of identity and the roles we use to organize these meanings. It is unwise to make decisions in these states of mind. A better solution is to review our memories and make plans in states when we can pay calm attention to details, reduce avoidance, and proceed slowly but reasonably to better future engagement with the world.

# 10
# Attitude
# Transformation

When defensiveness declines and we are in a calm state of mind, we can contemplate hard topics. Reappraising our ideas can change our attitudes, and those alterations increase maturity. I have discussed how to practice aspects of this process in each chapter. As a review, this chapter offers a longer example of an individual who was able to modify some of his concepts about himself and others.

I used the word transformation in the subtitle of this book. I did so because for me it meant two interwoven processes. One set of changes in self-organization involves largely interpersonal attitudes: I mean modifications in concepts of what has happened, is happening, and is likely in the future. These alterations involve expectations and intentions as well as prioritization of values and principles of right behavior. The autobiographical self has a new narrative as a result of such work.

The second set of changes harmonizes parts of self into a more coherent whole. In a way, this aspect of self-transformation is a matter of articulations between narratives, a form that emerges with more solidity, grounding, and smoothing of emotions. For example, the first set of changes may involve closeness and caring for others rather than envying or despising. The second, woven in, set of changes involves configuring the positive of caring with the negative attitudes. For example, one unconsciously remembers that a person who is now frustrating is a person who was and will be non-frustrating, that is rewarding to the self. This can relieve the chronic malaise of mixed anxiety and depression that Hank experienced.

## Hank

Hank, a man in his mid-30s, sought help from me for his persisting moods of depression and anxiety. He pined for love but had no enduring relationship. He felt inadequate in his search for what he wanted, his own wife and children. He also felt that his career suffered from a lack of productivity and success.

Hank had chosen law school because he liked the combination of acquiring knowledge and engaging in adversarial actions. He had graduated near the top of his class and was offered an associate position in a large, prestigious law firm. He hoped to eventually become a partner, but that would require competitive as well as cooperative successes.

During law school, Hank's aptitude indicated that he should be able to rise to high standing. He did apply himself to his studies, but he marred his academic success with procrastination. He could have been at the very top of his class, but his procrastination meant that often missed dotting every *i* and crossing every *t*. Essentially, he was brilliant but late. Now in the firm, Hank tried to work hard but met his deadlines only by staying up all night just before the due date.

His ambition to be promoted was thwarted by the fact that he could not make himself complete briefs in a timely manner. We aimed to find out why and began to look at his states of mind while at work. I encouraged him to be more patient in taking on the task of careful self-observations. We found that his attention often wandered from his current tasks. He might fantasize about his future sexual life while writing legal briefs. Conversely, while on a promising date, he might ruminate about the briefs from his current law work. Even when sticking to work on a legal problem, he flip-flopped between alternatives instead of comparing and contrasting them.

We were soon able to observe some repetitive self-states. Hank began his sessions by conversing about current events in a socially poised and confident stance. As we got into the emotional heart of the topic at hand, he grew tense, his speech became halting, and he often said something that he immediately tried to take back or undo. Hank labeled this self-state as *anxiously wavering*.

During one of our early sessions, I asked Hank to say more about what he wanted from himself at work. He said that he wanted to succeed by triumphing over adversaries. I asked whether competing with colleagues also brought up a fear of failure. Hank surprised me. He dreaded the possibility that he would experience intense *remorse* at having defeated and humiliated a rival. He imagined that a competitor could not lose without experiencing such a severe embarrassment that his self-confidence would be totally lost. Guilt over harming the rival with his success could overshadow any anticipated joy of victory. I told Hank that his attitudes seemed extreme.

Similar "top or bottom status" themes emerged in Hank's stories of relationships with women. In these stories, implicit attitudes became clearer and more explicit. Put into words, Hank felt that the man had to be the stronger partner, or else he would be foolishly subordinate. I told Hank that I noticed that equality, a balance between partners, seemed to be missing from his repertoire for relationships, both at work and in intimacies.

The insight that he carried in his mind too few models for cooperation helped Hank notice how he flip-flopped between extreme self-states, as either very strong or very weak, too strong or too weak. Without a balanced, "equal relationship" option, Hank alternated between strength and weakness with astonishing speed. He might start a sentence speaking about himself as a strong competitor seeking advancement at work, or beating a rival for the attention of a woman, but by midsentence, his adjectives switched and he began characterizing himself as too weak. He might begin and end a segment of discourse like this: "I am better at relating past legal decisions to current briefs than Ted, so I can . . . well, if not better . . . well, I guess I still have a lot to learn." Or he might say of his latest date, "I really felt great that she wanted to go out with me, but what have I got to offer a standup person like her? I don't know, maybe she will quickly reject me."

I looked for derivatives of these attitudes in our back-and-forth conversations. Hank might start to challenge me on the meaning and accuracy of one of my clarifications of an apparent pattern. He would then quickly change his mind about my error in the clarification and submit to its undoubted correctness and pertinence. As he went from a strong self-state to a weak one, he was in a self-state I labeled as *obsequiousness.* I floated out an idea: Could an inhibited, dangerous resentment be underlying his almost obedient stance? Was his weak self-presentation a way of undoing the boldness of disagreeing with me and feeling like he would beat me down?

Hank looked straight into my eyes with what I took as a glare. He said something general, and I replied, "What do you mean?" He began to debate my inquiry, sarcastically repeating, "What do you mean? What do you mean?"

I said to Hank, "Right now you seem angry at me for badgering you with questions that you find difficult to answer." Then Hank went from angry to calm. He shared with me a memory about his father badgering him cruelly by saying, "Why did you do that? *Why did you do that?*" Hank had felt belittled and quickly became remote, although inwardly angry. I had sounded like that to him, but on review, he could have equally well interpreted the tone of my questions as kind, inquisitive, and usefully persistent.

Hank learned a new attitude about us together in conversation. Hank came to understand my intentions in challenging him. He realized that I was not debasing him when I pointed out his problematic behaviors, but that I was encouraging him in his own careful self-observation. By learning that we were cooperating in alliance, he could unlearn some of the old winner/loser configurations and learn some models of equal exchanges. He modified the harshness of his inner critic — not, of course, in just one conversation, but in many.

Hank gradually learned to speak directly in an understandable, emotionally well-modulated way, even when he was talking about unpleasant topics. He made a consistent, conscious effort to address the emotional heart of a topic. He learned to stay on a topic initiated by me without feeling subjugated, and he came to feel safe disagreeing with me. He could change topics deliberately and appropriately without worrying about putting me down.

When I clarified to Hank his pattern of presenting himself in alternating weak and strong roles, he remembered how, as a child, he had feared that he would not develop enough strength to escape his domineering and sometimes frighteningly aggressive father. Staying close to his father was unacceptable because it implied that Hank would always remain the weaker party, never able to leave home or develop his manhood. Being remote from his father as a young boy felt too lonely and unsupervised. Seeing the historical pattern helped him clarify his current repetitive attitudes. This then helped him change so he could develop new patterns.

As Hank grew up, he was desperate to escape his father's firm grip, but he felt guilty whenever he succeeded in any capacity. He believed that, to become strong and independent, he would have to compete with or humiliate his father, who seemed to want the best for Hank, even though he was unempathic about what might be best for his son. During adolescence, Hank became taller and physically stronger, but his growth seemed to humiliate rather than please his father. Then Hank's father developed Parkinson's disease. Both Hank and his father irrationally believed that Hank's physical development of strength and athletic abilities had somehow diminished his father's power. Putting these childlike attitudes into words and reflecting upon them helped Hank see the irrationality. He retrospectively constructed a more reasonable narrative.

Getting a more adult perspective on this pattern from the past by putting the attitudes into clear words for the first time enabled Hank to notice ways in which his childhood pattern still organized some of his thoughts and actions. He still behaved as if he needed to either humiliate or submit to father figures in order to be strong and independent. His attitude of ingratiating submission was inappropriate to the actual situation because he was dealing with accomplished professionals who would not be threatened if Hank had a useful idea they had not yet formulated. Moreover, they wanted to see him grow in his own capacities as a lawyer.

Hank told me of adolescent fantasies that contained themes in which he emerged victorious from deadly conflicts. In adulthood, Hank tempered these themes, but he still viewed the trial lawyer role like a hero in combat and sought admiration for displays of his skill in "demolishing" the opinions and assertions of his adversaries. Preparing a subtle but incisive argument was his best way of showing off. Through such acts, he planned to gain status and surpass rivals, but he feared the summit and backed down before he could achieve it. His self-defeating pattern now seemed understandable and alterable. He could win a case and not kill an opponent.

What were Hank's unconscious attitudes before he changed his self-organization? Embedded in his beliefs about success was fear, and embedded in his ideas of enjoying the accomplishments of others was envy and hostility. When Hank was manifestly strong and assertive, he feared the effect his hostility would have on others, as if his success would harm them. He felt either guilty (over the suffering others had incurred from being defeated in competing with him) or fearful (of himself succumbing to their envious retaliation). Fear of retaliation was part of what caused his self-state of *anxiously wavering.*

In the course of transformation, Hank altered both his attitudes towards others when he felt himself in a stronger position than them, and when he felt himself in a weaker position. In both sets of attitudes the concept of harm was softened. In addition, he had better articulation of being strong with being weaker. This coherence was part of that softening of the dangers of aggression or competition.

What changed? At work, Hank began to recognize that equals might compete or even fight without the loser being destroyed or the winner being devastated by guilt. In his experiences with women, this recognition meant that both parties might be frustrated by each other without having to break up because of a transient frustration or irritation. His prior feelings of dismay at losing were replaced with new, less intense feelings of sorrow. He no longer irrationally expected that, when he competed vigorously and well, his success would harm his rival. He could savor occasional states of victorious joy from his triumphs in competitions, without switching to the guilt that he had fought too hard and harmed others. Hank still had periods of loneliness, apprehension, tension, and sadness, but these feelings were tolerable and transient because he had increased harmony in his self-organization. He had reduced habitual avoidances and increased his skills of reflective consciousness. In relationships, he expressed negative feelings in well-modulated ways, and he knew how to monitor and when to check negative emotional urges.

## *A New Perspective*

When I began my residency in psychiatry, and as I gained the knowledge and skills to treat and help patients, I gained the support of the experienced faculty members who worked with me. They encouraged me to look at the amazing properties of the human mind with a sense of wonder. Now, in my turn, I want to pass along this point of view.

In self-contemplation, an attitude of wonderment rather than self-distain can help you be kinder to yourself and to feel much more comfortable when you open up. A sense of awe can replace, or at least ameliorate, severe self-criticism. With this softer perspective, you can stay aware longer and be less likely to shut down under the stress that a passage of self-transformation may require.

So as you proceed on this adventure of self-discovery, I encourage you to give up the self-talk that says, "How could I have been so stupid?" and instead say to yourself, "Would you look at that! Isn't it amazing that I could believe and feel that way?"

I also encourage you to greet new ideas with friendly curiosity. Test every idea. Air all your intuitions. Brainstorm. Follow your hunches. Remember that even the most outrageous and "dangerous" idea might contain the seed of something that could be useful to you. Above all, avoid a doom-and-gloom mentality. Remaining realistic is not the same as subscribing to pessimism. Optimism and courage bolster self-confidence and motivate you to forge ahead. These qualities are not investments from cosmic forces or gifts bestowed on only a lucky few; they are virtues that can realistically be cultivated by anyone who wants to possess them and who is willing to do the work.

## Our Judging Minds

We all have a judging mind. Our internal dialogue lists all rights and wrongs, good and bad, and tells us how things "should" be. Sometimes it even judges its own tendency to judge — too harsh, too lenient, or just right? In the process of self-examination, the judging mind can be a great hindrance if it is too harsh or too lenient.

Recently, a friend told me about how difficult it was for him to deal with people who talk on cell phones, particularly on buses. When he overheard the conversation of passengers sitting near him, he became angry and critical of their lack of consideration. He felt superior in his high regard for those much more polite and civilized individuals who did *not* chat on a cell phone in public.

My friend recognized that this attitude was, in fact, just his mind running off in its judging state, as it was prone to do. "So I watched it and didn't suppress it," he told me. "And when I saw how quick it was to insult others, the mind-set lost its pull."

In certain moments, all of us can free ourselves from the inner struggle with our judging voice. Sometimes the voice of the judging mind is loudest when it is directed at one's self, and these are the moments when cultivating the powers of self-acceptance are essential. Judging yourself negatively for being as you are is like judging the moon, the weather, and the sea for ebbing and surging tides. Being kind to yourself and aware of your nature opens you to all the possible benefits of working through your attitudes.

## *Points to Remember*

- Shadows of the past are cast into how people view the present and future. Outmoded attitudes are hard to recognize in reflective consciousness because they are so familiar as aspects of self that they persist without change. We must make special effort to observe and reappraise them.

- Fresh interpretations of new and near future opportunities can give us more zest for life, because change can be both exciting and rewarding. Although it occurs slowly for most of us, it can occur — and that is a source of renewable hope.

# 11
# Finding Your True Self

Finding your true self involves aligning your relationship attitudes with what you think is right and wrong. That alignment can be a product of the kind of work we've discussed in this book. Finding it is not like prospecting and coming across the gold mine of a true unconscious self deposited within you by fate. You don't simply excavate a true self — you make it happen. Your true self is in the possible future.

My daughter works as a leadership coach, and I have sat in on her group sessions. During one conversation, the participants clearly wanted authenticity but did not know quite what that was. Their discussion clarified some common goals. Each group member wanted authenticity as an attribute of identity and wanted others to regard him or her as honest, meaningful, solid, and capable of really delivering what one offered to deliver.

Another word the group used was legitimacy. Legitimacy and authenticity seem like modern psychology words, since becoming an individual is now assigned high value. We want to become true selves, to develop both inner truth and coherence, in the context of being seen by others as worthy rather than deceitful, posturing, exaggerating, or manipulating.

When you have repeated the work we covered in earlier chapters, you have, to some extent, rewritten your autobiography and sorted out your goals for the near future. Next, you will behave differently and see where those new plans work well and where you encounter obstacles in fulfilling them. What will happen in the next act in your theater of life? You are empowered by hope, but you are also preparing to face any difficulties that arise. Let us consider a few such difficulties here.

## Finding Self in a Troubled Relationship or Dispiriting Work Environment

The poem *Invictus* has a memorable end: "I am the master of my fate, I am the captain of my soul." I like the sentiment of that so much that I memorized it when I was 17. Since then, I have noticed the related problem that not all relationships are secure, caring, empathic, and cooperative. When you are not well reflected by others, maintaining your own dignity is difficult. Becoming more harmonized, legitimate, and authentic then seems hard to even imagine.

You will encounter times when you are not well situated with others. You may need to work on imagining possible ways to improve the situation. In the theater of the mind, engaging in an imaginative play of alternatives allows you to envision future possibilities. Sometimes this imaginative play leads to totally unrealistic but mood-restorative fantasies. The use of fantasy in reaching such calming or pleasurable states leads to idealizing properties that we cannot really achieve. In terms of change, of course, this restorative fantasy life is a false solution: Visions of the future should not become too utopian. However, you can create an authentic, legitimate, possible self by considering both real limitations and real possibilities.

In this experience of "finding your true self," you will encounter obstacles. Overcoming them usually involves finding your new value priorities.

## Values

Values are a prologue to our lives. They predate our awareness. Our communities and families pour them into the fabric of our social lives and, thus, also into our minds.

Uncovering the unconscious values that guide our intuitive sense of right and wrong, and our tendency to follow certain rules and prohibitions, is part of becoming wise and mature. Our parents, extended families, spiritual and secular communities, and wide range of movies, TV shows, and books keep on confronting us with ideologies. From these offerings, we chose what values to take in as our own principles. These values guide us as we struggle with our impulses, urges, and resentments. But some of our choices were made earlier and without clear awareness by our child or adolescent minds. Reconsider these values now, as a reasoning, competent, adult who understandings complexity in social life and in adjusting inner life to that social life.

In drama, we examine characters of fiction to identify the kinds of characteristics we would like to find or avoid, either in ourselves or in those we hope to trust. Dramas teach us about possible characters. We can imagine from them possible true friends or lovers, as well as see the potentials in everyday life for deceit and betrayal. We can project from them characteristics to emulate or avoid as role models.

Dramas are not dramas if they do not contain complexity of character. We want to see people on stage like us — people who may have primitive urges to excel, beat down or retaliate; people occupied with jealousy, violent impulses, and thwarted creativity; and people looking for ways to connect with others. We watch dramas to find out how the characters handle these situations, and sometimes we learn from unconscious identifications with their good solutions to moral dilemmas. Theater is a help, not just an entertainment. From our imaginings in our inner theater of contemplative possibility, we need to choose what to actually do to express ourselves and behave with other people. Sometimes we need to correct or compensate for our previous lapses.

## Lapses

We all need to work toward balance, reason, and coherence. Use rational thinking and periodic reappraisals of your interactions with other people to do that work. This means facing up to the facts, including slip-ups and selfish mistakes. We all have work to do to be "true to our principles" by refining those principles, examining our cultural or community values, and remaining ever ready to learn.

Although it can be uncomfortable and embarrassing to think about your lapses, the process of examining your slip-ups can be a valuable learning experience. By taking an honest appraisal, making amends, performing acts of remorse, and planning how to avoid making the same mistake again, we can soften our embarrassment and earn a genuine sense of pride and self-respect.

Learning from lapses emphasizes conscious contemplation rather than efforts to shed blame and avoid the truth. Expanding our thinking allows us to arrive at new and perhaps creative solutions to old problems. If we learn to tolerate shame and guilt, we can use these feelings for self-motivation rather than self-flagellation. With good motives and reasonable plans, we can improve our relationships.

Look for a balance between extremes of finding yourself totally blameless (because others are at fault) or totally bad. Project into the future and think about what you *would* do in contrast to what you *did* do. Rehearse this new plan. When the time is right, carry it forward into action.

## Forgiveness

Just as we benefit from forgiving others their trespasses, we benefit from asking for forgiveness. In everyday life, this means making an apology. Apologizing appropriately and effectively is a skill. First, keep your eye on your aim to restore a good connection. Suppress any temptations to continue to express anger or place responsibility on someone else. Instead, highlight the values you share. Maintain your self-respect and personal boundaries.

You don't have to spill your guts in a huge confession, but you should explain your motives and give realistic assurance that you will behave differently in the future. Describe or negotiate any acts you will undertake to restore amicability or to make reparation. When you are apologizing to a child, keep in mind that you are being a role model and teaching the value of owning up to mistakes. You are teaching how to make amends.

Self-organization is largely unconscious. It is complex, with multiple layers. "Finding your true self" means putting these together as harmoniously as possible.

## Maintaining Your Identity

You can expect threats to your selfhood. The main five threats are 1) too continuously mourning a loss from the past, 2) anticipating a bleak future, 3) experiencing contradictions in part of yourself without harmonizing them, 4) feeling as if you are totally alone in the world, and 5) feeling so absorbed in a group that you lose your sense of identity. You can take actions to address any of the threats that apply to you. For example, instead of crying over spilt milk, you can focus on retaining valued connections with your past, even if you have been separated from some positive relationships.

### Retain the Past

Work on connecting to your roots, even if you disagree with some of them. A culture's laws and legends are meant to endure as part of individual character. That is why repetition is used to inculcate them. Even architecture of dwellings and meeting places contains symbols that share community identity. When these symbols are lost, as in war, dislocation, or neglect, a person may feel as if he or she has lost the past. For example, this may happen if a fire destroys a family's house and all its artifacts, such as photographs and memorabilia. In such cases, it's important to rebuild key memories and a sense of the past.

On the other hand, when the body is damaged, the past body image must be remembered as past but not present. Keeping up-to-date on how the body really works now is necessary. We can have an image, like a photograph of our high school prom, but we also need to know how we look now and see the connection. If we lose fingers through an accident, for example, we need to figure out how that hand can now work best and act to get there. In such an instance, we could take inspiration from a pianist who lost a right hand and subsequently wrote pieces for the left hand, to avoid having to give up music.

## Puzzle Through the Maze of Possible Futures

If you are alive, your future is not totally bleak. You do not know precisely what implications new learning may have for developing yourself and your relationships. Part of learning is letting the imagination of possibilities occur. We all need to face threats, but we do not want to succumb to loss of hope. If we have sustained a disability, we do not want to mourn a past self perpetually. Instead, we want to see the possibilities that lie before us.

## Harmonize Through Self-Expression

Contradictory values, needs, desires, fears, motives, goals, and roles exist in all of us, and we discussed ways to harmonize them in earlier chapters. That harmonization is helped when we put those contradictions in a reviewable form. Journals, notes, and plans provide for such review. Without attempting to make a career or money out of the product, one benefits from self-portraits, self-dancing, poems, and written memories. These expressions help consolidate identity and restore some stability even in a state of disturbed identity.

## Even When Alone, Plan How To Get Together

Being alone can decompose self and lead to a sense of identity disturbance. We have emphasized having a loving set of relationships, but even with such support, we may find ourselves isolated, stigmatized, or rejected. This is a kind of deprivation of self-reflection from others.

We can work to gain self-reflection from others, even when we have been abandoned, as we try to form new relationships by volunteering, working in teams, and displaying a pleasant demeanor to strangers (while being careful, of course). Sitting on a park bench, at a beach, or in a coffee shop puts us near other people. Doing so without conversing may initially feel like we are more painfully alone than if we were at home alone. Striving to tolerate the initial discomfort of being seen by others as alone or lonely is worth the effort because we can derive value from establishing eye contact or hearing voices in a small group.

## Maintain Identity in a Group: Stand on Your Own Feet, Sit on Your Own Bottom

A life of constant group occupancy and excessive connection can also lead to problems such as identity disturbances. The schema of group connection, like being in a chorus line, has been of value. But we also want the chance to fulfill a solo role, even if only for a few seconds in a long dance. Too little time alone results in less time to find a "true self." To keep from being totally absorbed by the group, take initiative in doing some aspect of familiar works and rituals while imagining other possible futures. Even if you are paid to do the chorus line number over and over, you can design your own dance in your free time and express yourself as the choreographer.

Most of us are not absorbed in a total institutional setting. However, we may be crowded, compelled to work in intense social situations and under tight control from supervisors for economic reasons or responsibility to a family. Learning to tolerate and like oneself when alone may be a skill to learn. Attitude is important. Self-talk such as "Now I have been abandoned" is not a good way to tolerate being alone. On the other hand, self-talk such as "Now I can relax with my book, or TV program, or music" is positive because it says, "I am the agent of what I do now," even if what you do is a respite from tension.

Ultimately, your true self is a kind of collage that you put together. When it seems disturbed, watch for the five threats just discussed and consider what to do about them. Each of us is a work in progress, with ourselves as writers of what "true" means in our search to become a true self. Our self can be made more coherent using reasoned and reflective thinking that includes attention to values and connections to others.

# ACKNOWLEDGEMENTS

My children Ariana, Jordan, and Joshua gave me examples and discussions that increased, I think, the vividness of my illustrations. My patients did this as well, and showed what transformations were possible even in difficult circumstances. I am grateful.

Margarite Salinas, Zack Vanderbilt, Jessica Sheer, Christopher Scott, Krista Hansing, Sherri Ortegren, and Renée Binder clarified and processed this manuscript ably and well. It would not be before your eyes without them. Thank you each.

I now feel like a creature of the University of California. I did my under and post-graduate training there, have been on the faculty for decades, and like Quasimodo, will probably be ringing the academic bells when I finish contributing by teaching. I love my alma mater and am deeply appreciative of the university as a concept, as well as the more direct contributions of my colleagues to the contents of this book.

# REFERENCES

Abend, S.M. (2005) *Analyzing intrapsychic conflict: Compromise formation as an organizing principle.* Psychoanalytic Quarterly. 74(1)5-25.

Adler N, Horowitz MJ, Garcia A, & Moyer A. (1998). *Additional validation of a scale to assess positive states of mind.* Psychosomatic Medicine, 60(1);26-32.

Ainsworth, M., Blehar, E. Waters, & Wall, S. (1978). *Patterns of attachment: A psychological study of the strange situation.* New York: Basic Books.

Ainsworth, M. (1973). *The development of infant-mother attachment.* In B. Caldwell and H. Ricciute, (Eds.), Review of Child Development Research, no. 3. Chicago: University of Chicago Press.

Baars, B.J. (1987). *A cognitive theory of consciousness.* London: Cambridge University Press.

Baars, B.J. 1987. *Biological implications of a global workspace theory of conscious experience.* In G. Greenberg and E. Tobach, eds., Language, Cognition, Consciousness: Integrative Levels. Hillsdale, NJ: Erlbaum.

Baars, B.J. 1987. *What is conscious in the control of action? A modern ideomotor theory of voluntary control.* In D. Gorfein and R.R. Hoffmann, eds., Memory and cognitive processes: The ebbinghaus centennial symposium. Hillsdale, NJ: Erlbaum.

Beattie H. 2005. *Revenge: A Panel Report.* Journal of the American Psychoanalytic Association (JAPA), Vol. 53(2), Spr pp. 513-524.

Beck, A. T. (1976). *Cognitive therapy and the emotional disorders.* New York, NY: International Universities Press.

Beck, A. T. & Alford, B. A. (2009) *Depression: Causes and treatments* (2<sup>nd</sup> ed). Philadelphia, PA: University of Pennsylvania Press.

Beck, A. T., Emery, G., & Greenberg, R. L. (2005) *Anxiety disorders and phobias: A cognitive perspective.* New York, NY: Basic Books.

Beck, A. T., Freeman, A., & Davis, D. D. (2003) *Cognitive therapy of personality disorders.* New York, NY: The Guilford Press.

Benjamin, L.S. (2003) *Interpersonal reconstructive therapy: promoting change in nonresponders.* New York, Guilford Press.

Berne, E. (1961). *Transactional analysis in psychotherapy.* New York: Grove Press.

Blackmore, Susan. 2004. *Consciousness: An introduction.* New York: Oxford University Press.

Blatt, S. 1990. *Interpersonal relatedness and self-definition: Two personality configurations and their implications for psychopathology and psychotherapy.* In J. Singer, ed., Repression and Dissociation: Implications for Personality Theory, Psychopathology, and Health. Chicago: University of Chicago Press. [Ch 3]

Blatt, S. J. (2004) *Experiences of depression: Theoretical research and clinical perspectives.* Washington, DC: American Psychological Association Press.

Boekhout, B.A, Hendrick, S.S. & Hendrick, C. (2003) *Exploring infidelity: Developing the relationship issues scale.* Journal of Loss and Trauma, 8:283-306.

Bowlby J. (1957). *An ethological approach to research in child development.* British Journal of Medical Psychology. 30,230-240.

Bowlby J. (1960) *Separation anxiety.* The International Journal of Psychoanalysis, 41:89-113.

Bowlby J. (1963). *Pathological mourning and childhood mourning.* Journal of the American Psycholoanalytic Association, 11(3):500-541.

Bowlby, J. 1969. *Attachment and loss, vol. 1: Attachment.* New York: Basic Books.

Bowlby, J. 1973. *Attachment and loss, vol. 2: Separation, anxiety and mourning.* New York: Basic Books.

Bowlby, J. 1980. *Attachment and loss,* vol. 3: *Loss, sadness and depression.* London: Hogarth.

Bowlby, J. (1992) *The making and breaking of affectional bonds.* London, UK: Routledge.

Bowlby J. (2004). *The role of childhood experience in cognitive disturbance.* In Freeman A, Mohoney MJ, Devito P, & Martin D (eds), Cognition and Psychotherapy ($2^{nd}$ ed.) pp. 101-121. New York, NY: Springer Publishing Co.

Brenner, C. (2006). *Psychoanalysis or mind and meaning.* New York: Edited by The Psychoanalalytic Quarterly

Bretherton, I., & Waters, E. (Eds.). (1985). *Growing points in attachment theory and research: monographs of the society for research in child development.*

Britton, R. (2003). *Sex, death, and the superego-*

*experiences in psychoanalysis.* New York: Kamac.

Byron: (2004) *Testotorone Inc: Tales of CEOs gone wild.* NY: Wiley & Sons

Calarge, C., Andreasen, N.C., & O'Leary, D.S. (2003). *Visualizing how one brain understands another: A pet study of theory of mind.* Am J Psychiatry, 160, 1954-1964.

Caldwell, L. (2007) *Winnicott and the psychoanalytic tradition.* Karnac, London.

Calhoun, LG & Tedeschi RG, Edited by (2006) *Handbook of posttraumatic growth: Research and practice.* Routledge

Castonguay, L. G., Newman, M. G., Borkovec, T. D., Holtforth, M. G.,& Maramba, G. G. (2005). *Cognitive-behavioral assimilative integration.* In J. C. Norcross & M. R. Goldfried, (Eds.), Handbook of Psychotherapy Integration, 2nd ed., (pp. 241-260). New York: Oxford University Press.

Clarkin, J. F., Yeomans, F. E., Kernberg, O.F. (2006). *Psychotherapy for borderline personality: Focusing on object relations.* Arlington, VA: American Psychiatric Pub Inc.

Cloninger, CF: 2004. *Feeling good: The science of well-being.* New York, Oxford University Press.

Colarusso, C. A. & Nemiroff, R. A. (1981). *Adult development: A new dimension in psychodynamic theory and practice.* New York, NY: Plenum Press.

K L Critchfield; J F Clarkin; K N Levy; O F Kernberg. *Organization of co-occurring axis II features in borderline personality disorder.* British journal of Clinical Psychology, 47, Part 2 (2008): 185-200

de Maat, Saskia; de Jonghe, Frans; Schoevers, Robert; and Dekker, Jack. (2009) *The effectiveness of long-term psychoanalytic therapy: A systematic review of empirical studies.* Harv Rev Psychiatry 17:1-23.

Dyer KF, Dorahy MJ, Hamilton G, Corry M, Shannon M, MacSherry A, McRobert G, Elder R, McElhill B: *Anger, aggression, and self-harm in PTSD and Complex PTSD.* Journal of Clinical Psychology, 65(10)1-16, 2009.

Edwards, V.J., Holden, G.W., Felitti, V.J., & Anda, R.F. (2003). *Relationship between multiple forms of childhood maltreatment and adult mental health in community respondents: Results from the adverse childhood experiences study.* Am J Psychiatry. 160: 1453-1460.

Eells, T.D. (2007) *Handbook of psychotherapy case formulation*, second ed., New York: Guilford Press.

Eisnitz, A. (1986). *The perspective of the self representation in dreams.* In A. Rothstein, ed., The Significance of the Interpretation of Dreams in Clinical Practice. New York: American Psychoanalytic Association Press.

Ekman, P. (1984). *Expression and the nature of emotion.* In P. Ekman and K. Sherer, eds., Approaches to Emotion. New York: Erlbaum.

Emde, R. N., and J. F. Sorce. (1983). *Rewards of infancy: Emotional availability and maternal referencing.* In J. Coll, E. Galenson, & R. Tyson, (Eds.), Frontiers of Infant Psychiatry. New York: Basic Books.

Emde, R. N. (1988) *Development terminable and interminable: I. Innate and motivational factors from infancy.* International Journal of Psycho-Analysis *69*, 23-42.

Erikson, E. H. (1950). *Childhood and society*. New York: W.W. Norton.

Erikson, E. H. (1956). *Problem of ego identity*. Journal of the American Psychoanalytic Association 4, 56-121.

Erikson, E.H. (1959). *Identity and the life cycle*. In Psychological Issues. New York: International Universities Press.

Erikson, E.H. (1962). *Young man luther: A study in psychoanalysis and history*. W.W. Norton & Co., Inc.: New York, NY.

Fairbairn, W. R. D. (1954). *An object relations theory of the personality*. New York: Basic Books.

Foa, E.B., Keane, T., Friedman, M. and Cohen, J. Editors. (2009). *Effective treatments for PTSD: Practice guidelines from the international society for traumatic stress studies*. 2nd Edition. NY: Guilford Press.

Fonagy, P., & Target, M. (2003). *Psychoanalytic theories: perspectives from developmental psychopathology*, London: Wiley.

Fonagy, P., & Target, M. (2003). *Being mindful of minds: A homage to the contributions of a child-analytic genius.* Psychoanalytic Study of the Child, *58*, 307-321.

Fonagy, P., Roth, A. & Higgit, A. (2005) *Psychodynamic psychotherapies: Evidence-based practice and clinical wisdom.* Bulletin of the Menninger Clinic, 69(1), 1-58.

Freud, S. (1900). *The interpretation of dreams.* In Standard edition, vol. 3. London: Hogarth Press.

Freud, (1901-1905). *Oedipus complex. Three essays on infantile sexuality and other works.* In J. Strachey, The Standard Edition of the Complete Psychological Works of Sigmund Freud, Vol. VII. The Hogarth Press and the Institute of Psychoanalysis, London, England.

Freud, S. (1903). *On psychoanalysis.* In Standard Edition, vol. 12. London: Hogarth Press.

Freud, S. (1905). *Three essays on the theory of sexuality.* In Standard Edition, vol. 7. London: Hogarth Press.

Freud, S. (1913 [1911]). *On psycho- analysis.* In J. Strachey, The Standard Edition of the Complete Psychological Works of Sigmund Freud, Vol. XII. The Hogarth Press and the Institute of Psychoanalysis, London, England.

Freud, S. (1911-1915 [1915]) *The dynamics of transference.* In J. Strachey, The Standard Edition of the Complete Psychological Works of Sigmund Freud, Vol. XII. The Hogarth Press and the Institute of Psychoanalysis, London, England.

Freud, S. (1920). *Beyond the pleasure principle.* In Standard Edition, vol. 18. London: Hogarth Press.

Freud S. *The ego and id.* In The Standard Edition of the Complete Psychological Works of Sigmund Freud, vol 17. Edited by Strachey J. London, Hogarth Press, 1955 (original work published 1923).

Furlong, A. (2009) *Love sickness, love and temporality*, *JAPA* 57:1071-1096

Gabbard, G. O. (2005) *Mind, brain, and personality disorders.* American Journal of Psychiatry, 162, 648-655.

Gedo, J., & A.Goldberg. (1973). *Models of the mind.* Chicago: University of Chicago Press.

Goldberg A. (2007) *Moral Stealth.* Chicago: University of Chicago Press.

Greenberg, J.R., and Mitchell, S.A. (1983). *Object relations in psychoanalytic theory.* Cambridge, MA: Harvard University Press.

Greenson, R.R. (1967). *The Technique and Practice of Psychoanalysis.* New York: International Universities Press.

Greenspan, SI, McWilliams, N, Wallerstein, R. (2006) *The psychodynamic diagnostic manual* (PDM).

Grotstein, J. S. (1981). *Splitting and projective identification.* New York: Jason Aronson.

Hartmann, H. (1964). *Essays on ego psychology: Selected problems in psychoanalytic theory.* New York:

Hedges, L.E. (2003). *Listening perspectives in psychotherapy, 20th Anniversary ed.,* by Lawrence E. Hedges. New York, Jason Aronson.

Horowitz, M. J. (1976/1986). *Stress response syndromes, 1st & 2nd eds.* Northvale, N.J.: Jason Aronson.

Horowitz, M.J. (1979) *States of mind.* New York, NY: Plenum.

Horowitz, M.J. (1984) *Personality styles and brief psychotherapy.* New York, NY: Basic Books.

Horowitz, M.J. (1987) *States of mind: Configurational analysis of individual psychology.* New York, NY: Plenum.

Horowitz MJ, (1988). *Formulation of states of mind in psychotherapy*. American Journal of Psychotherapy; 42(4):514-520.

Horowitz, M.J., ed. 1988. *Psychodynamics and cognition*. Chicago: University of Chicago Press.

Horowitz, M.J. 1988. *Introduction to psychodynamics: A new synthesis*. New York: Basic Books.

Horowitz, M.J. (1991) *Hysterical personality style and the hstrionic personality disorder*. 2nd edition. Northvale, NJ, and London: Aronson.

Horowitz, M.J. 1992. *Psychic structure and the processes of change*. In M.J. Horowitz, ed., Hysterical Personality Style and the Histrionic Personality Disorder. 2nd ed. Northvale, NJ: Jason Aronson.

Horowitz, M.J. (1991) *Person schemas and maladaptive interpersonal patterns*. Chicago: University of Chicago Press.

Horowitz, MJ. (1997) *Formulation as a basis for planning psychotherapy treatment*. Washington, DC: American Psychiatric Press, Inc.

Horowitz, MJ. (1998) *Cognitive psychodynamics: From conflict to character*. New York, NY: Wiley.

Horowitz MJ, (1998). *Personality disorder diagnosis*. The American Journal of Psychiatry; 155(10).

Horowitz, M.J. (2003) *Treatment of stress response syndromes*. Washington, DC: American Psychiatric Publishing, Inc.

Horowitz, M. J. (2005). *Understanding psychotherapy change: A practical guide to configurational analysis*. Washington, DC: American Psychological Assoc

Horowitz, M.J. (2007). *Understanding and ameliorating revenge fantasies in psychotherapy*. Am J Psychiatry 164(1):24-27.

Horowitz, M.J. (2009) *A course in happiness*. NY: Pengiun Group.

Horowitz MJ. (2009). *Value reprioritization in psychoanalysis*. Journal of the American Psychoanalytic Association; 57(6):1361-1377. Doi: 10.177/0003065109353335.

Horowitz MJ, Adler N, and Kegeles S. (1988). *Narcissistic rage in leaders: The intersection of individual dynamics and group process*. International Journal of Social Psychiatry, 34(2), 135-141.

Horowitz, M.J., Kernberg, O., and Weinshel, E. (eds.) (1993). *Psychic structure and change in psychoanalysis*. New York: International Universities Press.

Horowitz, M.J., C. Marmar, J. Krupnick, N. Wilner, N. Kaltreider, and R. Wallerstein. 1984. *Personality styles and brief psychotherapy*. New York: Basic Books.

Horz S.; Mertens W.; Stern B.; Caligor E.; Critchfield K.; Kernberg O.F.; Clarkin J.F. *A prototypical profile of borderline personality organization using the structured interview of personality organization (STIPO)*. Journal of the American Psychoanalytic Association, v57 n6 (2009 12 01): 1464-1468.

Horowitz MJ, Milbrath C, Bononno GA, Field N, Stinson C, & Holen A. (1998). *Predictors of complicated grief*. Journal of Personal and Interpersonal Loss; 3(3):257-269.

Horowitz, M.J., Milbrath, C., Ewert, M., Sonneborn, D. & Stinson, C.H. (1994) *Cyclical patterns of states of mind in psychotherapy*. American Journal of Psychiatry *151* (12):1767-1770

Horowitz, M.J., Milbrath, C., Jordan, D., Stinson, C.H., Ewert, M., Redington, D.J., Fridhandler, B., Reidbord, S.P., & Hartley, D. (1994) *Expressive and defensive behavior during discourse on unresolved topics: A single case study.* Journal of Personality 62 (4): 527-563.

Horowitz, M., Milbrath, C., & Stinson, C. *Signs of defensive control locate conflicted topics in discourse.* Archives of General Psychiatry 52: 1040-1057, 1995.

Horowitz, M.J., Stinson, C., Curtis, D., Ewert, M., Redington, D., Singer, J., Bucci, W., Mergenthaler, E., & Milbrath, C. (1993) *Topics and signs: Defensive control of emotional expression.* Journal of Consulting and Clinical Psychology 61:421-430,

Horwitz, A.V. and Wakefield, IC. 2007. *The loss of sadness: How psychiatry transformed normal sorrow into depressive disorders.* N.Y.: Oxford Univ. Press.

Ikemoto, T. (1996). *Thesis research: Moral education in Japan; Implications for American schools.* Retrieved July 19, 2004, from http://www.hi-ho.ne.jp/taku77/papers/thes595.htm

Jacobson, E. 1964. *The self in the object world.* New York: International Universities Press.

Jones E, Bumming J, and Horowitz M. (1988). *Another look at the nonspecific hypothesis of therapeutic effectiveness.* Journal of Consulting and Clinical Psychology, 56(1), 48-55.

Jung, C. G. (1933). *Modern man in search of a soul.* New York: Harcourt.

Jung, C.G. 1959. *The archetypes and the collective unconscious.* New York: Pantheon.

Kachele, (Kachele) Horst; Schachter, Joseph; Thomas, Helmut: (2009) *The ulm psychoanalytic process research study group.* New York, London: Routledge, 470 pp.

Kagan, J., and A. Moss. 1983. *Birth to maturity.* New Haven: Yale.

Kendler, KS and Prescott, CA: 2006. *Genes, environment, and psychopathology: Understanding the causes of psychiatric and substance use disorders.* N.Y.: Guilford.

Kernberg, O.F. 1976. *Object relations theory and clinical psychoanalysis.* New York: Aronson.

Kernberg, O.F. 1980. *Internal world and external reality: Object relations theory applied.* New York: Jason Aronson.

Kernberg, O.F. 1967. *Borderline personality organization.* Journal of the American Psychoanalytic Association 15:41-68.

Kernberg, O.F. 1975. *Borderline conditions and pathological narcissism.* Northvale, NJ: Jason Aronson.

Kernberg, O.F. 1982. *Self, ego, affects, and drives.* Journal of American Psychoanalytic Association 30:893-917.

Kernberg, O.F. (1987) *An ego psychology-object relations theory approach to the transference.* Psychoanal Q. 56(1):197-221.

Kernberg, O. F. 1992. *Aggression in personality disorders and perversions.* New Haven, CT: Yale University Press.

Klein, M. (1957). *Envy and gratitude: A study of unconscious forces.* New York: Basic Books.

Klein, G.S. 1976. *Psychoanalytic theory.* New York: International Universities Press. [Ch 3]

Klein, M. (1940). *Mourning and its relation to manic-depressive states.* Int. J. Psycho-Anal., 21:125-153.

Klein, M. 1948. *Contributions to psychoanalysis.* London: Hogarth Press.

Klein, G.S. 1976. *Psychoanalytic theory.* New York: International Universities Press.

Kohut, H. 1972. *Thoughts on narcissism and narcissistic rage.* Psychoanalytic Study of the Child 27:360-400.

Kohut, H. 1977. *Restoration of the self.* New York: International Universities Press.

Kohut, H. (1984). *How does analysis cure?* In A. Goldberg and P. Stepansky, eds., Contributions to the Psychology of the Self. Chicago: University of Chicago Press.

La Farge L. 2006. *The wish for revenge.* Psychoanal Q, 75(2):447-75

Langer, E. (1983). *The psychology of control.* Beverly Hills, CA: Sage.

Langer EJ: *Rethinking the role of thought in social interaction.* In Harvey J, Ickes W, Kidd R (eds), New Directions in Attribution Research, Vol 2. Hillsdale, NJ, Erlbaum, 1978

Langer, S. 1951. *Philosophy in a new key.* New York: Mentor Press.

Levinson, D. 1978. *The seasons of a man's life.* New York: Ballantine Books. [Ch 3]

Linden M. 2003. *Posttraumatic embitterment disorder.* Psychother Psychosom, Jul-Aug, 72(4):195-202.

Luborsky, L. (1984*). Principles of psychoanalytic psychotherapy: A manual for supportive-expressive (SE) treatment.* New York: Basic Books.

Luborsky, L. & Crits-Christoph, P. (1990). *Understanding transference: The CCRT method.* New York: Basic Books.

Maercker A, Bonanno G, Znoj H, & Horowitz M. (1998). *Prediction of complicated grief by positive and negative theses in narratives.* Journal of clinical Psychology; 54(8):1117-1136.

Maerchker, Andreas; Einsle, Franziska; Koller, Volker. (2007). *Adjustment disorders as stress response syndromes: A new diagnostic concept and its exploration in a medical sample.* Psychopathology, 40:135-146.

Main, M. (1975). *Mother-avoiding babies.* Paper presented at biennial meeting of Society for Research in Child Development, April.

Makari, G. *Revolution in mind: The creation of psychoanalysis.* New York: Harper Perennial, 2009.

Mandler, G.A. (1975). *Mind and emotion.* New York: Wiley & Sons.

Mandler, G.A. (1985). *Cognitive psychology: An essay in cognitive science.* Hillsdale, NJ: Erlbaum.

Masterson, J. F. (1979). *The splitting defense mechanism of the borderline adolescent: Developmental and clinical aspects.* In J. E. Mack, (Ed.), Borderline States in Psychiatry (pp. 93-101). New York: Grune and Stratton.

Masterson, J. (2000). *The personality disorders.* Phoenix, AZ: Zeig Tucker & Theisen Inc.

Mitchell, S.A. (1988). *Relational concepts in psychoanalysis.* Cambridge, MA: Harvard University.

Murray, H. A. (1938) *Explorations in personality.* New York: Oxford University Press.

Norcross, J. C., & Goldfried, M. R. (2005). *Handbook of psychotherapy integration,* 2nd ed., (Eds.) J. C. Norcross, & M. R. Goldfried. New York: Oxford University Press.

Ogden, C.K., & Richard, I.A.: 1923. *The meaning of meaning.* New York: Harcourt Brace.

Ornstein, P. (1986). *On self state dreams.* In A. Rothstein, ed., *The significance of the interpretation of dreams in clinical work.* New York: American Psychoanalytic Association Press.

Panksepp, J. (1982) *Toward a general psychobiological theory of emotions.* Behavioral and Brain Sciences. 5:407-422, Cambridge University Press.

Perry J, Hoglend P, Shear K, Vaillant G, Horowitz M, Kardos M, et al. (1998). *Field trial of a diagnostic axis for defense mechanisms for DSM-IV.* Journal of Personality Disorders, 12(1):56-68.

Peterfreund, E. 1971. *Information, systems, and psychoanalysis: An evolutionary biological approach to psychoanalytic theory.* Psychological Issues 7 (1/2). Monograph 25/26.

Posner MI, Rothbert MK, Vizueta N, Thomas KM, Levy KN, Fossella J, Silbersweig D, Stern E, Clarkin J, Kernberg OF (2003) *An approach to the psychobiology of personality disorders.* Dev Psychopathol 15:1093-106.

Rapaport, D. (1967). *Cognitive structures.* In M. Gill, ed., Collected Papers of David Rapaport. New York: Basic Books.

Renick, O. (2006). *Practical psychoanalysis for therapists and patients.* New York: Other Press.

Schank, R., and R. Abelson. 1977. *Scripts, plans, goals and understanding.* Hillsdale, NJ: Erlbaum.

Segal, Z.V., Williams, J.M.G., Teasdale, J.D. (2002) *Mindfulness-based cognitive therapy for depression: A new approach to preventing relapse.* New York: Guilford Press. pp. 351

Silberschatz G. (Ed.) *Transformative relationships: The control mastery theory of psychotherapy.* New York, NY: Routledge, 2005

Singer, J.L. (1966). *Daydreaming.* New York: Random House. Psychodynamics and Cognition, pp. 297-346. Chicago: University of Chicago Press.

Slap, J. W., and A. J. Saykin. (1983). *The schema: Basic concept in a nonmetapsychological model of the mind.* Psychoanalysis and Contemporary Thought 6:305-325.

Sroufe, L.A., and Fleeson, J. (1986). *Attachment and the construction of relationships.* In W. P. Hartup & Z. Rubin, (Eds.), Relationships and development. Hillsdale, NJ: Erlbaum.

Stern D. N: (1998). *The process of therapeutic change involving implicit knowledge: Some implications of developmental observations for adult psychotherapy.* Infant Mental Health Journal. Special Issue: Interventions that affect change in psychotherapy: A model based on infant research. 19(3), 300-308.

Stern, D. N. (2004) *The present moment: In psychotherapy and everyday life.* Norton Series on Interpersonal Neurobiology. New York, NY: W. W. Norton & Co.

Stevens, A. 1982. *Archetypes: A natural history of the self.* New York: Morrow.

Stolorow, R. D., and Lachmann, F. M. (1980). *The psychoanalysis of developmental arrests.* New York: International Universities Press.

Stricker, G., & Gold, J. (2005). *Assimilative psychodynamic psychotherapy.* In J. C. Norcross & M. R. Goldfried (Eds.), Handbook of Psychotherapy Integration, 2$^{nd}$ ed., (pp. 221-240). New York: Oxford University Press.

Strupp, H.H., & Binder, J.L. (1984). *Psychotherapy in a new key: A guide to time-limited dynamic psychotherapy.* New York, NY: Basic Books.

Symington, N. 1986. *The analytic experience.* New York: St. Martin's Press.

Thickstun, J.T., and A.D. Rosenblatt. 1977. *Modern psychoanalytic concepts in a general psychology.* New York: International Universities Press.

Tomkins, S.S. (1962). *Affect, imagery, consciousness, vol. 1: The positive affects.* New York: Springer.

Tomkins, S.S. 1979. *Script theory: Differential magnification of affects.* In H.E. Howe, Jr., and R.A. Dienstbier, eds., Nebraska Symposium on Motivation, 1978, vol. 26, pp. 201-236. Lincoln: University of Nebraska Press.

Vaillant, G. E. (1977). *Adaptation to life.* Boston: Little-Brown.

Van Pragg, H.M., de Kloet R., & van Os J. (2004) *Stress. the brain and depression.* Cambridge, U.K., Cambridge University Press.

Viney, T. (1969). *Self: The history of a concept.* Journal of the History of Behavioral Sciences 5:349-359.

Wallerstein, R.S. (1983). *Defenses, defense mechanisms, and the structure of the mind.* Journal of the American Psychoanalytic Association 31(5):201-225.

Wallerstein, R.S. 1986. *Forty-two lives in treatment: A study of psychoanalysis and psychotherapy.* New York: Guilford Press.

Weiss, J. (1967). *The integration of defenses.* International Journal of Psycho-Analysis 48:520-524.

Weiss J, & Sampson H. (Eds.) (1986). *The psychoanalytic process: Theory, clinical observation and empirical research.* New York: Guilford Press.

Winnicott, D.W. (1989) *Psychoanalytic exploration.* Harvard University Press, Cambridge.

Wurmser, L. (1981). *The mask of shame.* Baltimore: Johns Hopkins Press.

Young, J. (1999) *Cognitive therapy for personality disorders: A schema-focused approach*, 3rd ed., Sarasota, FL: Professional Resource Press.

Young J. E., Klosko, J. S., & Weishaar, M. E. (2003). *Schema therapy: A practitioner's guide.* New York, NY: Guilford Press.

Made in the USA
Charleston, SC
14 August 2012